Leander Edmund Whipple

The philosophy of mental healing;

A practical exposition of natural restorative power

Leander Edmund Whipple

The philosophy of mental healing;
A practical exposition of natural restorative power

ISBN/EAN: 9783337814632

Printed in Europe, USA, Canada, Australia, Japan

Cover: Foto ©ninafisch / pixelio.de

More available books at **www.hansebooks.com**

THE PHILOSOPHY

OF

MENTAL HEALING

A PRACTICAL EXPOSITION OF
NATURAL RESTORATIVE POWER

BY

LEANDER EDMUND WHIPPLE

NEW YORK
THE METAPHYSICAL PUBLISHING COMPANY
1893

COPYRIGHT 1893
BY
THE METAPHYSICAL PUBLISHING COMPANY.

PREFACE.

DURING the years in which the curative influence of mental practice has been demonstrated, there has developed a quiet yet earnest appreciation of the importance of the work. This is naturally expressed in a constantly increasing demand for some book which will give a correct idea of what Mental Healing is, and what may reasonably be expected to result from an understanding of its principles. To meet this growing demand for information of a practical nature, the present volume has been prepared, with the belief that the results of experience must prove of value to earnest inquirers.

In planning its scope and entering into the detail of explanation, it is recognized that the subject will be new to many readers, and that in some instances the established facts will run counter to accepted theories of life, even as the results of practice contrast with the consequences of acting upon more familiar theories. Also, that the usages of language necessary for intelligible explanation of metaphysical principles are in a measure unfamiliar to those who have not made these principles a study; therefore, those usages can not be strictly adhered to without detracting from the usefulness of the book.

The subject deals minutely with nearly every field of mental research, and to explain each point in detail would require a volume of such proportions that few would find it available; indeed, it is so extensive and so absorbingly interesting that the temptation to become voluminous in explanation of either theory or practice is almost irresistible. In view of these considerations, and in order that the present work may cover the broadest field of usefulness, it becomes important that it should be somewhat limited in extent, yet of sufficient clearness to convey to those unfamiliar with the nomenclature not only a correct impression of the Ideas involved, but of their practical value to humanity.

The principal aim has been to present concisely those ideas most important to a general understanding of the natural relation existing between life and health, together with an explanation of the laws which render Mental Healing possible. Another purpose has been to set forth the *demonstrated facts* of Metaphysical Healing, in such a manner that inquiring minds may be enabled personally to examine, through the experiences of those around them, some of the common lines of mental action in which proofs are obtainable that mind both causes and cures disease. Successfully to accomplish all this in one small volume is no simple task, and a consideration of the difficulties involved will insure the indulgence of the critical reader.

No claim is made to original conception of idea with regard to the theory of cure by mental influence exerted through the imaging faculty. Though practically new to Western thinkers, this idea, in some form or other, has existed for centuries in the Orient. It has also been demonstrated and taught to a moderate extent by some of those interested in the Mental Healing movement for the past thirty years; yet its importance seems to have been underrated, and it appears to have been frequently set aside in favor of theories offering greater allurements—theories which, perhaps, appeal more to the emotions than to the faculties of intelligence exerted through intellectual and scientific thought.

The claim made for this work is, that it presents—though in a form necessarily limited—the results of experience derived from many years of constant study of mental influences and their physical effects, in a practice of wide extent, maintained among people of the highest grades of intelligence, where the action of mind could be observed in all its varying phases.

The most careful and painstaking tests have been made of all modes of mental action met with, and of their various correspondences in the physical system. This study has been conducted without bias of any sort, and with the one purpose always foremost: to extract from amidst the mass of conflicting theories and of confusing testimony frequently advanced, the fundamental truth of the Mental Healing movement— a truth so evident in many of its results of practice. This investigation has developed facts of human existence heretofore unrecognized by modern thinkers, and principles of life-action not generally taught even in the advanced Schools of Mental Healing.

Careful study shows that the Imaging Faculty of Mind is the instrument of human existence. This being true, it follows that only through the natural laws by which Mind images Ideas can any real mode of action in human life become established. On examination, this statement proves to be a Truth that withstands every form of honest investigation—the hotter the fire, the brighter and purer the metal which emerges from the flames.

The writer entertains the opinion that Absolute Truth can safely invite any amount of careful investigation, together with the most thorough and accurate tests that can be applied through logic, reason and philosophical thought, or in scientific experiment of the most accurate description; in fact, the closer such investigation keeps to actual facts, the more staunch and immovable stands the idea under examination, provided it be the Truth.

So-called Truth which depends upon an effervescing, emotional sentiment for either recognition or practical application, will vanish as soon as its effervescence has reached the natural limit of its simulated action; and a "Truth" which must be taken on the statement of others, because it will not bear independent investigation, has no attractions for any thinker capable of appropriating and bringing into useful development the *facts* of universal reality.

Extended explanation of the various topics of each subject contained within this philosophy will be given in separate works calculated to deal with each subject independently in so far as is found practicable. It is thought, however, that the present volume may prove valuable as an introduction to all lines of study of this really inexhaustible subject, by means of the explanation given of *Mental Action and its natural physical effect*, which is the key to many of the mysteries of human existence.

L. E. W.

New York, August, 1893.

The Philosophy of Mental Healing.

CONTENTS.

		PAGE
PREFACE,		iii

I. METAPHYSICAL HEALING:
Its Nature and Scope, 13

II. METAPHYSICS *versus* HYPNOTISM:
Is Mind Cure Mesmerism? 34

III. THE POTENCY OF METAPHYSICS IN SURGERY:
Does Mental Healing Claim to Replace Surgery? 47

IV. THE PROGRESS OF THE AGE:
Universal Ether and Telepathy, . 59

V. INTELLIGENCE AND SENSATION:
The Office of the Senses, . . 75

VI. MENTAL ACTION:
The Process of Thought, 87

VII. THE PHYSICAL REFLECTION OF THOUGHT:
Its Expression on the Body, . 101

		PAGE
VIII.	THE MENTAL ORIGIN OF DISEASE:	
	Thought Images,	115
IX.	CURATIVE INFLUENCES:	
	What is a Mental Cure? .	129
X.	THE PHYSICAL EFFECTS OF ANGER:	
	How Mental Action Causes Disease, .	144
XI.	THE INFLUENCE OF FEAR IN SICKNESS:	
	Discordant Emotion and its Results, .	155
XII.	ILLUSTRATIVE CASES:	
	Cures that have been Effected,	171
XIII.	CURES THAT HAVE BEEN EFFECTED (Contin'd).	
	Various Effects of Fright, .	181
XIV.	MUSCULAR and INFLAMMATORY CONDITIONS:	
	Heart Disease, Fevers and Colds,	195
XV.	THE COMMON GROUND OF HEALING METHODS:	
	Why do Conflicting Theories Heal? .	209
XVI.	CONCLUSION:	
	The Importance of the Movement,	225

THE

PHILOSOPHY OF MENTAL HEALING.

CHAPTER I.

METAPHYSICAL HEALING.

Its Nature and Scope.

AMONG the questions arising in the mind of every investigator of this subject, the following are perhaps oftenest asked, because most important to an intelligent comprehension of the scope and importance of the movement:

1. What is Metaphysical Healing?
2. In what sense is it metaphysical?
3. What knowledge is the basis of the theory?
4. What benefits are likely to result from an understanding of the principles?

5. Has it any foundation in Science, Philosophy, Logic or Reason?

6. Are the theory and working power capable of scientific demonstration?

7. Will the knowledge be of permanent benefit to man?

8. Will any harm result from the practice?

Clear and correct answers to these questions are of vital importance to those who wish to understand the manifold phases of human existence. In these times of varying opinion, diverging views and contradictory theories, life's problem frequently seems more than ever difficult to understand; but, in fact, the increased activity of mind which is expressed in diversified thought, leads to extended research, which is clearing up many obscure subjects and bringing to light hidden mines of knowledge. This frequently develops resources of the human mind heretofore unrealized. One important result is a re-discovery of the healing power which inheres in rightly regulated thought-action, and which is now presented under the head of Metaphysical Healing.

Metaphysical Healing is a mental method of establishing health, through an understanding of the fundamental principles of Being or universal Life and the working laws of its activities. It is commonly known as Mental Healing, and (under various theories, more or less perfect in construction) is popularly spoken of as Mind Cure.

The various schools of Mental Healing are based upon practically the same fundamental principles. They differ in theory, chiefly because the principles being universal in scope, and therefore infinite in extent and variety, are beyond full comprehension in finite thought—hence they are recognized in various degrees of understanding.

The character of the Principle to be considered is of first importance; the name employed in description of the work is important only to the extent that it should be accurately descriptive of the nature of the principles involved in the healing act.

The term Metaphysical Healing is derived from the English noun Metaphysics. It is employed here because Metaphysics is the only word that, in scope, covers every form of those activities of life which make an act of healing possible to the human mind. It correctly describes both the principle and its action, and accurately names the theory on which the healing power is based. The following are standard definitions of the word:

"Metaphysics is the science of Being." "The science of the conceptions and relations which are necessarily implied to be true of every kind of Being—philosophy in general; the science of first principles."

"Metaphysics is the science of the first principles of Being; the science of the first principles of knowledge, and the science of the beginning and the end of all things—the absolute unity of Being and Thought."*

"Metaphysics is the science which deals with the principles which are presupposed in all Being and Knowing."

"The beginnings of Science and of Metaphysics are identical; although there is a sense in which Metaphysics comes before the Scientific era."†

Metaphysics is mathematical, therefore exact; knowledge of its principles is, necessarily, scientific understanding. Mathematics, also, is metaphysical, and underlies all real law in the universe. DeQuincey says: "Mathematics has not a foot to stand upon which is not purely metaphysical." "All parts of knowledge have their origin in Metaphysics and finally, perhaps, revolve into it."

Knowledge of Being, in any of its forms, is strictly metaphysical, also mathematical, in its nature. Conscious understanding of any definite law of life is knowledge of that part of Being; for every real Law

---
*Aristotle.   †Encyclopædia Britannica.

and every true Principle is an active, living part of Being itself. The Principle is the living entity, while the corresponding Law is its expression. Through the activity of Law the energy of Principle is manifested: healthy, living action is the natural result.

There are no new laws of Being; there is only discovery of law by those to whom that subject is new. If the theory advanced be rightly founded upon first principles, it is a part of the one Science of Being and accurately deals with the corresponding laws: for Science is only a concise name for knowledge of law, and Being means living, essential principle.

Every metaphysical principle has some direct bearing upon the activities of life, thereby affecting the health of the human race. A theory of healing established upon these principles must be metaphysical in character; therefore, the application of acquired knowledge of principles and laws of life to the act of healing becomes a "special metaphysics," accurately described by the term Metaphysical Healing.

The Method of metaphysical healing is based upon the laws which govern the intelligent side of human nature. In various degrees of activity this includes the intellectual, thinking and reasoning faculties of mind, the intuitive faculties of the soul, and the perceptive faculties of the spiritual nature.

The Philosophy of metaphysical healing deals with the elements and activities of human nature on all planes of existence, beginning with sense-evidence and leading up through intellectual comprehension, logical reasoning and the intuition of the soul to pure spiritual perception of the fundamental principles of Being. The universal information thereby gained develops an understanding of humanity in all phases of life. This is essential to a knowledge of how to remedy the ills that flesh has been supposed to be heir to, but which proceed mostly from man's misunderstanding of his own nature.

This line of investigation, properly pursued, will give a clear knowledge in detail of the principal activities of the physical body, of the relation existing between mind and body, including the action of the individual mind both upon its own body and upon other minds, and of Mental Activities on the moral plane, so far as may be necessary in order that a healthy state of both body and mind may be established in natural harmony. This prepares a right foundation for the still higher development of those faculties of the spiritual nature of every individual, which frequently lie almost dormant underneath the accumulation of materialistic opinions of an opposite character.

Investigation of Mental Activities has been conducted with quite as thorough and painstaking earnestness as the physician employs in examination of the physical structure, or as the scientist in any material line devotes to his particular subject. By this means fresh acts are constantly brought to the surface and the knowledge becomes extended.

The practical theory of Metaphysical Healing may be stated as follows: Proceeding naturally from the Fundamental Principles of Being, there are definite Universal Laws of mental activity through which the movements of physical bodies are always regulated. These laws are fundamental to all modes of physical action and to life on any objective plane.

Mind—the intelligent, thinking and reasoning Individual—is a living entity organized upon these principles and laws, in accordance with which it acts and reacts in thought and perception, outwardly and inwardly, in unison with the Fundamental Principles of the universe. By individual compliance with these laws, results in harmonious and healthy action are outwardly expressed through natural law on the physical body, as well as on the minds of others who enter the same field of activity.

Through intelligent understanding, these laws are accessible and, if understood, the influence will be correct, producing results which must be harmonious and healthy. If not understood, wrong action is probable, and correspondingly discordant results in the life of that individual are absolutely certain, regardless of intention; because, mental action contrary to the laws of universal life, whether it be intentional or accidental, conscious or otherwise, is not in harmony with the mathematical exactness of fundamental principles, therefore is discordant in character, producing outward results of distress, which vary in intensity with the degree of departure from exact law.

These results may be attributed to various external agencies, but really they are the natural outcome of mental action maintained in erroneous channels. The only right remedy is a change in the course of the mental action involved. Power to effect this change for another rests solely in knowledge of the fundamental Principles of Being and their working laws. Comprehension of these facts leads to the following reply to our opening questions:

1st. What is Metaphysical Healing?

Metaphysical Healing is a mental method of establishing health through knowledge of the principles of Metaphysics. The principles of Metaphysics are the permanent laws of the universe, therefore they are the underlying laws of human existence.

2d. In what sense is it metaphysical?

It is metaphysical in the sense that every step in its practice is taken in exact accordance with some definite fundamental principle of the living activities of Being. Being is the active, conscious reality of the universe.

3d. What knowledge is the basis of the theory?

The theory is based upon knowledge of those Laws which are fundamental to human life, and which in repeated tests prove to be the same for all individuals, varying only in degree of intensity, never failing or becoming inoperative while life remains.

4th. What benefits are likely to result from an understanding of the principles involved in Metaphysical Healing?

(a.) Through knowledge of the various activities of conscious life, gained by a full understanding of the philosophy of Metaphysical Healing, it is possible to learn the underlying cause of any form or degree of sickness—mental, moral or physical. By the natural force of properly directed Thought-energy, this cause may be removed without the agency of opiate, stimulant or any injurious process.

With such assistance, those who are sick from any cause may be restored to health and natural duration of life by a return to the harmony of the natural action of both body and mind, provided that a cure is still possible in that case by any means. Experience proves that myriads of cases heretofore considered incurable may be permanently cured by means of metaphysical understanding of the facts of life's experience, when dealt with by an understanding mind, under suitable conditions for natural restoration.

Discords known as physical diseases have their origin in mal-action of some of the natural functions of the system, which in turn are under direct control of the mental mechanism. By establishing correct mental activity, the wrong action is changed to a right one in both the mental and the physical organisms, and the disease is undermined.

(b.) New energy and activity enter with the understanding of causes and reasons, and moral tendencies are quickened. Both mental and spiritual faculties become more active, and natural abilities are correspondingly increased in power for action. This develops the best qualities possible to that individual mind.

Parents, guardians, nurses, and all who have charge of the education of children and the care of invalids or others, find the understanding of Natural Law to be the most efficient help in management. Those in possession of such knowledge, properly applied, attain a degree of success that is otherwise impossible.

(c.) The intemperate, who wish to reform and who will, to a reasonable extent, co-operate with the metaphysician, are assisted in the most effective way by removal of the original cause of the desire for a stimulant, after which the unnatural appetite vanishes and the sufferer recovers his normal condition of health and happiness. Metaphysical Healing will soon be known as the real remedy for the hitherto unconquerable malady, Intemperance, because it strikes at the root of the evil, which has been discovered in no other philosophy.

5th. Has Metaphysical Healing any foundation in Science, Philosophy, Logic or Reason?

(a.) Science. The word Science literally means knowledge of fundamental law. The foundation of Metaphysical Healing rests upon Science, because it is based on theoretical knowledge of principles, and the healing theory is constructed on definite understanding of the active laws which proceed from those principles. No feature of any theory is accepted as final until it has been proved and demonstrated, without possibility of disproof and without an instance of failure, when it can be applied under the exact conditions which are necessary for a fair test of any scientific problem. It is, of course, equally important that the test should be conducted by one capable of examining with scientific comprehension.

(b.) Logic. Metaphysical Healing is logical in character, because the action is a process of thought, in "classification, judgment, pure reasoning and systematic arrangement of ideas," bearing upon those laws and principles of life which relate to health, considered in their direct bearing upon a given case. A correct treatment is a pure, formal process of thought based upon comprehension of the principles involved in the condition requiring to be changed.

"Pure logic is the true form or formal laws of thinking; applied logic teaches the application of the forms of thinking to those objects about which we think." In metaphysical practice, applied logic is employed while dealing with Ideas and forming thought processes to produce healthy results.

(c.) Reason. Logical reasoning leads the mind upward through intellectual process to the higher planes of activity, where principles are comprehended. The conclusive act of pure metaphysical treatment is a clear comprehension of the Principles of Life involved in the case under treatment.

(d.) Philosophy. Metaphysical Healing is a philosophy of existence, because it deals with the phenomena of life as explained by and resolved into "causes and reasons, powers and laws," with regard to both sickness and health, showing the active causes of sickness, teaching the fundamental laws of health, and explaining the reason for each action in life. The true metaphysician makes a constant study of these Laws and bases his calculations on their rules, logically reasoning from one to the other, until the Fundamental Principles are reached and comprehended.

Philosophy has been defined as "The science of effects by their causes." Metaphysical Healing considers every sickness to be an effect, mathematically determines the cause which rests in the original wrong mental action, accidental or otherwise; obliterates it by causing that action to cease, and establishes a mental action of an opposite character in the place thereof. In this way sickness is replaced by health, on the mental plane, from which it was originally reflected and re-enacted in the physical mechanism.

"Philosophy is the science of things deduced from first principles." In metaphysical diagnostication for causes of evident effects, one deals through reason, with the fundamental principles of the life-activities of the patient. Through this process the real seat of the trouble is reached and a final conclusion arrived at, which, if rightly followed out, will result in permanent eradication of the harmful effect on both the mental and the physical planes. The line of logical reasoning and comprehension of principles which renders this act possible must eventually result in a Philosophy of Life and a Science of Healing, alike logical, reasonable, certain, safe, and universal in application.

6th. Is the theory and working power of Metaphysical Healing capable of scientific demonstration?

The theory of Metaphysical Healing is based upon eternal principles of Truth—actual verities: not material but spiritual in essence; therefore they must be spiritually examined. The practical field of operation for such examination can be reached only through intellectual comprehension of the facts of Law, which leads eventually to direct perception of Principles, on the plane of real consciousness above that of physical sensation. Here the details of theory may be examined as directly as can any object on the physical plane, and thus may be actually known, though directly provable only to one who has recognized and learned to use the instruments required for spiritual manipulation of principles.

The working power of Metaphysical Healing can neither be pulverized in a mortar, applied as a poultice, nor hypodermically injected; it cannot be swallowed, handled or microscopically examined; yet it proceeds from a true theory, possessing exact proportions, capable of precise delineation in metaphysical terms to those who are suitably prepared to examine principles on their own ground.

The theory is outwardly demonstrated, and the existence of its principles made known to the world through power of action upon the human mind, and to those who require sense-evidence, more especially in its power for healing physical ailments. In this field of action the physical change of tissue that will follow rightly directed mental effort, gives ocular demonstration of possible physical results from metaphysical action.

It is possible to so examine this process as to eliminate every possibility of an external reason for the resultant changes, and to repeat the process in successive experiments until the fact that physical change can be produced through mental action, unaided, is proved as absolutely as the well-known fact that oxygen and hydrogen, combined on a definite base of mathematical principle, will produce water, although neither of the fundamental elements when examined separately bears the least seeming relation to water.

The universal importance of Mathematical Principle in the construction and continuance of the Universe is demonstrated in the fact that the relation of water to oxygen and hydrogen does not exist under any other condition than the definite mathematical formula H_2O. The least variation from this exact proportion renders the formula inoperative. This is equally true of every physical element —even of the material universe itself. Mathematical Principle is the vital essence of every constructed thing and of every element.

The knowledge gained by adequate examination of the laws of mental action is equally scientific with the knowledge of chemical laws, the cause for the action of which no chemist can explain, though the action and its accompanying force are known to exist. Not only is the working power of Metaphysical Healing thereby proved, but the truth of the theory from which definite power is repeatedly produced, is also demonstrated with equal exactness.

7th. Will the knowledge of Metaphysical Healing be of permanent benefit to man?

That which results in changes at the foundation, bringing forward fundamental principles of life and causing the individual to conform his actions to them, must inevitably result in permanent good; because a *true idea* once aroused in mind can never be lost, but remains forever a part of that mind which has conceived the eternal fact of its living principle, regardless of the immediate act of conscious memory. The spiritual essence of that Idea has become a part of the living substance of that Individuality—this is individual development.

Because erroneous opinions are devoid of fundamental principle, they may be eradicated; but a true Idea once comprehended is forever incorporated in the understanding, resulting in permanent development for that individual, which can never be overthrown. Comprehension of metaphysical principles must result in advancement, which will inevitably reflect in improved action on the moral, the intellectual, and eventually, on the physical plane of that individual's life.

8th. Will harm result from the practice of Metaphysical Healing?

The pure application of metaphysical principles can never harm, or result in any but good and beneficial acts, because it is based upon and proceeds directly from genuine principles of eternal truth and perpetual good, which are necessarily pure both in character and in the result of their action. Darkness can never proceed from light, because it is not contained therein.

One who seems to produce evil effects by act of thought is not working with principles, therefore is incapable of producing metaphysical results. Principles are the only Verities of the universe; consequently, he is not dealing with Reality and can produce no permanently effective result; indeed, no result whatever can be so produced without either conscious consent or sub-conscious willingness on the part of the recipient to unite in activity which is contrary to the nature of principles. With adequate knowledge, each intelligent mind may be its own guide, guard and defender in all similar action.

Thought-action, to be permanent, must be true—that is, according to Principles. To be according to principles, it must be a clear, conscious apprehension of the principles of Reality. Such thought, when active in one mind, sends an outward current of this realization into the mental atmosphere, where it is inhaled or absorbed by others; only good influence can proceed from such activity.

True thought-action leads to Realization, not to Desire. The thinker who yields to evil inclinations and aims to harm another, follows self-desire, which is devoid of principle, and utterly fails to realize any true Idea. In willful selfishness he blindly hopes for action contrary to Law; such action would be devoid of living principle or essential quality, therefore unreal, inoperative and abortive in the end. He willfully desires but fails to realize; therefore, he accomplishes nothing real or enduring.

Lacking Realization, imagination is not an enduring mental act, therefore not a real thought. Possessing realization of principle, it is true, therefore real and necessarily good; for only Reality can be realized in the true sense of the word, and only that which is good can possess genuine principle of Reality. The essential quality of reality is good: its action necessarily must be good and the result harmonious. The good and the true are eternal, and may be permanently realized. Evil has no fundamental principle of living Reality, and cannot perpetuate itself. It possesses no real quality—no eternal essence; its only definite characteristic is its own native nothingness, and its only existence is in false imagination.

Discord is deceptive under certain circumstances, but unreal; no harm can come from it except to him who believes its falsity to be truth; even then the result proceeds from the undemonstrated opinion, not from any actual entity, and it only expresses the falsity of the opinion. Knowledge of law proves a safeguard here, and is a complete protection. Wrongly inclined thought can harm no one who knows the true laws, and through their exercise lives in the principles of harmonious Being. Metaphysical thought-action can never result in harm under any circumstances.

All enduring Principle is one eternal whole of essential reality. All permanent Law is one perpetual harmony of living activity. Every thought based upon realization of eternal principle is a real and lawful activity, essentially good in its nature. It is an active element of pure goodness which, when projected by one mind, is capable of being seen, heard or felt by others. These in turn become its thinkers, and pass it along to those who, through ready willingness to learn and know that which is true in the universe, are receptive to its harmonious influence in endless succession of progressive action, just as a pebble falling in a body of water starts a rippling circle outward, which, though unperceived in its journey, will end only where no water is to respond in undulations—where there is no element in which its action can be registered.

Knowledge of metaphysical principles is equally important to every member of the human family: for the comfort, even the continuance of the physical life of each one here, is certain some day to hinge upon the understanding of some one or more of the universal principles which are common to the life of every individual.

Principles are no respecters of persons, but they teem with the goodness of life, which is equally free to every living soul as is the light and warmth of the noonday sun. Each has but to rightly seek, in order to find and be able to lawfully appropriate his unlimited share of the inexhaustible supply of Universal Reality.

One living water of good perpetually bubbles forth from the eternal fountain of essential reality. Realization gives possession.

CHAPTER II.

METAPHYSICS versus HYPNOTISM.

Is Mind Cure Mesmerism?

THE advent and success of mental methods of healing have called attention to the fact that some influence other than medical can be beneficially exerted in sickness, resulting in the conviction that mind can act directly upon mind, without the intervention of the physical senses. Scientific investigation in various quarters of the globe has forced this conclusion, and the existence of an influence, at least not purely physical, now must be acknowledged by those who would recognize the progress of the age.

To some thinkers the theories of mesmerism seem to offer the most plausible explanation of the various phenomena of mental healing.

The power of mesmeric influence has been generally denied, and its practice condemned, by many who were supposed to understand its ground, since it was first brought to notice by Mesmer, in Vienna, in 1776. Extended experiment has proved, however, that power rests in that particular phase of mental action to a greater extent than has generally been admitted. This having been proved, the subject demands recognition and a suitable classification among the powers of the human mind.

The name *Mesmerism* had fallen into disrepute because of general condemnation of the subject and the word *Hypnotism*, with which the public are not quite so familiar, appears to have been adopted as a new garment for the old subject. Under this name the theory that the will of one person may be controlled by exercise of willful determination on the part of another, is rapidly becoming an established fact with medical men of all schools, and is now considered as possessing some degree of curative influence.

Until the nature and extent of mental action is understood, it seems easier to comprehend a mental influence which is supposed to be exerted through a means which is physical in part, than one attributed to a purely mental agency. This may account for the frequency with which we hear the question: Is Mental Healing Mesmerism or Hypnotism?

Occasionally the statement is seen in print over the signature of some one claiming authoritative information, that mind cure—what there is to it—is only a form, or feature of Hypnotism, and that eventually it will disappear in that "science."

No greater mistake can be made than to suppose that the active influence of Metaphysical Healing, or of any real mental cure, is applied through the same modes of action which govern the influence now being exercised in hypnotic experiment. Those who make this assertion are either incorrectly informed as to the real nature of mental cure, or they are unacquainted with the curative influence of metaphysical principles when exerted through the action of intelligent understanding;—perhaps, unacquainted with the principles themselves.

The English word Hypnotism is derived from the Greek ὕπνος, meaning sleep, particularly an abnormal or somnambulistic sleep, seemingly induced by external means;—a state of trance or some degree of insensibility to surroundings.

During hypnotic influence the subject surrenders his will to that of the operator, who thereupon takes possession of the mental mechanism of the submissive victim and does with it what he chooses, while the subject acts according to the will of the other, neither knowing what he does nor caring for results. This is the brutal control of one personality by another, without either moral element or agency. The action takes place entirely upon the lowest mental plane, that of the animal will—the brute plane of human life, where animal tendencies prevail. Its resultant action is a downward moral tendency for both subject and operator; neither can tell where the tendency will cease.

The Hypnotic Subject unconditionally surrenders his personality to the dictates of another, ceases to exercise his own faculties, and is temporarily without will, determination, moral or physical sensibility, choice, desire or power for independent action in any direction whatever. The operator acts through the mental mechanism of the subject, exercising control over the physical mechanism also, by the action of animal will. If the subject yields to this influence, he for the time being becomes practically non-existent except as the operator permits him to exist in imitative act.

Will is here falsely placed above Intelligence—a position which cannot be permanently maintained. The force exerted is limited in action to the extent of animal will, which possesses much less power than is usually supposed. The limit of the animal will is reached before that of any other of the mental faculties.

The moral side of this question will not be discussed here, further than to suggest that there is moral degradation in the unconditional surrender of one personality to the willful control of another at any time, in any manner or under any circumstances; and no rightly-informed person, unless he is to some extent morally degraded, would consent to deprive another of independent action for any other purpose than to save life or to do some great good not to to be performed in any other way.

In metaphysical treatment, however, an influence of an entirely different character is brought to bear upon the subject. No willful control of the patient occurs at any time or under any circumstances. If personal control, or self-will power, is exerted, the act is unmetaphysical, and the operator not a true metaphysician.

The patient is left at all times in the utmost freedom of possession of all his mental faculties; indeed, this freedom is always cultivated as the most desirable condition for effective mental treatment.

Metaphysical treatment is based upon the Intelligence instead of the Will. Intelligence is considered of first importance, because it is a higher faculty than Will, purer in character and more powerful in action. Even on the highest plane of spiritual action, where the higher element of divine will in man's constitution is the instrument of action, the will is entirely subservient to Intelligence.

Metaphysics appeals to spiritual faculty rather than to animal impulse. It speaks through intelligent understanding of the principles of Being, to the spiritual intelligence of the human soul, presenting to that Intelligent Individual the facts of his own existence for super-conscious consideration, and on them he may or may not act receptively, as he intelligently decides for himself. In this manner Metaphysics instructs, and metaphysical healing guides the wanderer out of the path in which he suffers, into a higher path of understanding, leaving the will free and untrammeled that it may develop to higher degrees of intelligent activity.

Truths are presented mentally which the individual may receive or reject with perfect freedom; an attempt to force him into undesired paths would render the act abortive, because Intelligence never forces except through the shedding of Light, and light brightens, rather than beclouds the intellect—it quickens, but never stupefies either faculty or function. Metaphysical influence elevates both intellectually and morally; it can never by any possibility degrade.

No good result can be produced through hypnotic control, even under the most favorable circumstances, which cannot be produced with greater benefit through an adequate knowledge of Metaphysics, and without the dangerous features, both moral and physical, that invariably attend the surrender of will and conscious intelligence.

Comparison of Hypnotic and Metaphysical influence may be made as follows: Hypnotism is a mental influence based upon the act of overpowering the animal will, which is the lowest degree of mental determination, or choice of action, and its power for action rests entirely with this one limitation of man's mental nature, while Metaphysical Healing is a mental act based upon spiritual intelligence, and covers the entire mental and spiritual nature, including the element of Divine Will—which is the only real element of will. The power proceeds from intelligent comprehension of the principles of the universe; this comprehension includes all true power for mental action.

When the nature of hypnotism is fully understood, its present feature of a willful control of one by another on the self plane will be eliminated, and man's real power for mental action will be recognized; that power is a loving guidance—by means of intelligent understanding—of the element of Divine Will which inheres in the real nature of every Individual. Then all selfish purpose will disappear and the power of hypnotism, now so astonishing, will be increased a thousandfold; its present disagreeable name and character will vanish, and its power for good will have merged into the parent power—intelligent understanding of the laws of Being—rightly named, Metaphysics. When this is accomplished the branch will be justly recognized as an active part of the living tree, from which it sprang and on which it must depend for further existence. The present methods of hypnotism lead downwards, and, if continued, must end in disaster to the theories and final annihilation.

Recent accounts of hypnotic experiments made in France mention achievements in the diagnosis of difficult cases, in which mental causes of disease were discovered by means of awakened memory on the part of the subjects, while in hypnotic trance. In one instance the subject recounted the details of an incident in childhood, which was considered a mental cause of her sickness. This cause was rendered quiescent, for the time being, by stating to her while in the trance state, that which the operator desired her to believe about the occurrence. This was considered necessary and justifiable because of the ends to be attained.

If there were no other way possible of giving relief, this might, perhaps, seem justifiable; but, as a matter of fact, the result obtained by this means is only the most feeble kind of a repetition of that which Mental Cure has been doing for many years, and has successfully accomplished in thousands of instances, both as regards the diagnosis and the cure, without any interference with perfectly free action of will on the part of the patient, without trance or any unnatural condition, and entirely independent of any hypnotic or mesmeric influence whatever.

Moreover, metaphysical understanding of the principles involved, enables the operator to permanently efface the troublesome element of fear or mental emotion which caused the disease, by causing the mental image to disintegrate, fade and vanish, while consciously speaking the truth in regard to it and knowing why the statements are true. This is one advantage possessed by the higher branch of the healing art.

In metaphysical diagnostication, similar mental causes, often fifty, sixty, seventy or more years past in life are brought forward in the memory—sometimes by questioning, at other times, where conscious memory does not work with clearness, by intelligent treatment which clears the mental faculties and freshens the memory; and instances are not uncommon in which they have been discovered psychically, without volition or conscious memory on the part of either the operator or the patient.

Metaphysical Healing has several ways of reaching the mental causes of sickness, any of which is better than hypnotic trance, because more natural and entirely harmless, while equally effective and absolutely permanent, with no possible chance for undesirable complications. Metaphysics strikes at the root of every harmful mental influence and annihilates it without danger or injury to any faculty.

Metaphysics encourages, while Hypnotism suppresses, intelligence on the part of its subject. Because of this fact metaphysical healing in every branch invariably meets its greatest success with the most intelligent people, in the most intellectual and spiritual families; while business and professional people of marked mental ability, strengthened by the power of intelligent comprehension of principles, are the most susceptible to its healing and restoring influence. The greater the degree of intelligence the more prompt and effective the response to treatment, and restoration to health.

On the other hand it is notorious that Hypnotism and all external mesmeric influences, find their most submissive subjects among the uncultured and mentally inactive. The subservient invariably prove the best subjects for hypnotic experiment. This is because a submissive will is necessary to a pliant hypnotic subject, while intelligent mental activity is incompatible with willing submission to unjust influence. Intellectual power renders one rightly independent and unsubmissive to selfish personal dictation, under all circumstances and in all degrees of consciousness.

In hypnotic experiment the subject must submit, either consciously or sub-consciously, to the willful act of the operator, before any appreciable degree of control can be exerted. It is because of this fact that under experiment so many people prove poor hypnotic subjects. No intelligent individual can be hypnotized or mesmerized *against* his will when properly exercised,—or without his own consent. This statement holds absolutely true with regard to direct influence when the subject is present with the operator; in the case of absent influence it will be equally true if the subject be naturally independent and intellectually active in assertion of his own higher will, through knowledge of the laws of real being, and alert to recognize influences which it is required to counteract. Knowledge is an absolute protection;—the hypnotic act is powerless without some degree of compliance on the part of the subject.

In metaphysical treatment appeal is made to the Individual Intelligence, and ideas that have been proved the facts of universal life are presented for intellectual comprehension on the higher plane of mentality, where the finest and best of human faculties are exercised, and where Fundamental Truths will be recognized on presentation. On this plane of consciousness the patient is always within reach of the guiding influence of right thoughts in regard to the activities of his own life.

Because of these Principles, metaphysicians, to be universally successful, must be honest and conscientious; rightly, not morbidly sympathetic, possessing clear intellectual comprehension of the affairs of human life, together with pure understanding of the spiritual side of human nature as expressed in the Divine Will, the good influence of which man shares in common with all Being.

If we recognize these facts, it is easy to understand that it is not, as frequently supposed, the mentally feeble, the weak, vacillating mortal, the imaginative, credulous or cranky specimen of humanity,—neither is it necessarily the inexperienced, the unsophisticated, the ignorant, or the least important member of the human family that is the most susceptible to the influence of metaphysical healing, but quite the reverse.

Metaphysics appeals most powerfully to the greatest minds, building an adamantine tower of understanding on a rock foundation of fact; while Hypnotism, even in the highest acts of its present aspect is, comparatively, but the plaything of children in the sand. A dangerous plaything, at that—a two-edged tool, dagger-pointed at either end.

Principles rule activities. Right eventually prevails.

CHAPTER III.

THE POTENCY OF METAPHYSICS IN SURGERY.

Does Mental Healing Claim to Replace Surgery?

THE relation of the subject of Metaphysical Healing to the practice of surgery in regard to its possible efficiency in cases of physical injury, is a question which frequently arises. The most common opinion is that in cases of a physical nature, mental influence must be inoperative, because it is not supposed either that mind was in any way involved in the affair that caused the injury, or that it can have any influence on the present physical condition. Some entirely erroneous opinions on this subject are frequently expressed by those who have not been correctly informed either with regard to the scope of mental action, or the position in which metaphysicians stand on the question.

The opinion seems to be somewhat prevalent that to affirm a mental cure is to proclaim a miracle.

This thought sometimes leads to the conclusion that if the professor is sincere, he must consider himself the possessor of miraculous powers, and it is inferred that he will claim the ability to perform impossible acts, regardless of natural law.

Direct questions repeatedly asked, by people of apparent intelligence, show that the following absurdities are supposed to be entertained by mental healers:

1. If the bone of a limb be fractured, one has only to think it is all right and he can walk or exercise the limb and recover without setting the bone.

2. If one chooses he can with impunity drink his coffee with arsenic instead of sugar, flourishing, meanwhile, on the unnatural diet.

3. If an eye be destroyed he has but to assert that he sees just as well without it as with it, and another eye will grow in the socket.

4. If the carotid artery be severed, thinking will stop the hemorrhage and restore the original condition.

5. If one only thinks so, he can lift a four-story house as easily as he can lift an orange.

6. The dead may be restored to this life, regardless of the condition of the body.

7. If mind controls the body, one may continue in the present existence forever.

Those who hold these absurdities usually entertain some such notion as that food, drink, air and sleep should be unnecessary to one who has the power to heal through thought, and if he should sneeze, cough, yawn, rest, exercise or enjoy himself in any natural way, he thereby proves himself to be an impostor.

These and kindred absurdities are based upon the one assumption that ability to perform miracles is postulated of the power to heal through act of mind. This notion is without foundation either in reliable metaphysical instruction or practice; the claim never proceeds from a metaphysical mind.

No class of thinkers have a deeper appreciation of the importance of natural law in human experience than rightly trained metaphysicians, whose entire study is of law and principle.

What might be done through sufficient information with regard to all the higher principles of the universe, is not the most important question for immediate consideration, but rather, what may be accomplished here and now, through accessible knowledge of universal laws. This is the problem which metaphysicians are called upon to solve for the immediate good of suffering humanity. When this has been accomplished, and the knowledge concentrated for effective action, higher dgrees of understanding may properly be aspired to, and will then be comprehended; but, he who leaps for the top round of the ladder first is apt, in falling short, to become tangled among the rungs nearer the ground which were at first ignored, but would better have been used as a foundation for sure climbing.

Everything that actually takes place under any circumstances is proved natural by the fact that it does take place, and it prevails only because of the existence of perfectly natural laws of that kind and quality. The investigator who neglects study of those laws will fail in every trying position.

If an act seems to be supernatural, it is only because this is the observer's first conscious experience with the law involved; when he becomes acquainted with its modes of action, its seemingly supernatural character will vanish, and it will receive suitable classification with nature's legitimate transactions.

There are no miracles;—the word is a misnomer. That which occurs in lines of action beyond present comprehension of natural law, has been called a miraculous act, and supposed to have been performed without regard to either universal laws or principles.

Any act, however simple, seems a miracle until accounted for by natural law; that instant its miraculous character vanishes. Our electric light would seem supernatural to an inhabitant of darkest Africa, unacquainted with the laws of electricity; yet to us it is a simple fact, easily accounted for on a natural plane of lawful activity.

If it be proved that an entirely new kind of power has been recently exerted, producing action hitherto unaccounted for, therefore impossible by any known law of activity, then the very fact that it has occurred at once establishes this mode of action as one of the existing laws of the universe, not previously recognized, perhaps, but a law nevertheless, else it could not have been in action.

If we say this is not law, but a special act performed without dependence upon, and contrary to law, we thereby postulate a lawless operator, destitute of principle, and in the ultimate, devoid of Being; because if there is no law in an action there is no principle behind it, and if no principle no Being; for Being is the Essential Principle of the universe and of everything in it. Without principle, neither Being, nor act of Being, is conceivable, in the light of the true meaning of both terms.

Continued investigation invariably demonstrates the natural character of every divine act. When the thinker masters the details of that species of activity, with the mechanism sufficient for its manipulation, he has at his own command the once miraculous power. Thus that which yesterday was considered miraculous or supernatural, is to-day perfectly natural and may be lucidly explained—while that which to-day still seems a miracle, to-morrow perhaps, will be recognized as the simplest of nature's playful acts.

Knowledge of the laws of Being shows all possible action to be natural, because it proceeds from the laws themselves; therefore no power whatever can be exerted by any intelligence, save through the action of some law, in expression of the quality of some one of the Principles of Being.

The real part of every Entity is its Principle. Only this can act at any time or for any purpose. A principle can act only by expressing its Quality, and this in turn can be accomplished only through the Law which exists for that purpose; therefore all expression of the quality of any principle must be, and invariably is, natural lawful action. With adequate comprehension of the principles involved, the true character of the act will be recognized.

The fact is, that Nature—Universal Mind—has yet in store myriads of modes of natural action and innumerable degrees of power, with which the human individual is as yet unacquainted. Man has been gradually learning these ways and the laws thereof, from the beginning. At every period he has considered all visible action that was beyond his comprehension, as the result of miraculous intervention in a supernatural manner on the part of some superhuman being. This is the history of the growth of human comprehension in all ages and among all classes.

Many laws of action in the universe, that were formerly unknown, are now understood; consequently, many acts have become possible to the human mind that were impossible before the acquirement of that knowledge. Mental healing is one of the advanced degrees of power that has developed from this understanding—the Knowledge and the Power go hand in hand. The same laws are involved in all conditions, both mental and physical, though the details of action are different.

The knowledge which gives power to heal diseased conditions, also makes it possible to relieve all unnatural conditions. In surgical cases distinct results may be produced by the removal of mental distress, fear, anxiety, worry, grief, pain and every degree of agitation, all of which are obstructions to nature's restorative processes and help to delay recovery. By no means the least of these results is the power to remove the particular impression of fear, fright, and mental or nervous shock which was produced at the time of the accident, and which frequently delays recovery because it continues active subconsciously in the mind of the patient, regardless of memory.

Mental assistance in quieting fear is legitimate metaphysical work, which is in some degree valuable in every surgical case. Mental Healing readily accomplishes this result, frees the mind of agitation and restores natural action in every part of the system, by removing mental obstructions to recovery, thereby rendering to nature the only advantageous assistance possible.

Under right mental conditions bones knit more rapidly and firmly, flesh heals in a fraction of the time usually claimed to be necessary, and scars are less prominent because of rapid natural activity during the healing process. Fever is reduced or avoided in both pulse and temperature, and suppuration is reduced to the minimum of natural restorative process. Liability to blood poisoning is also lessened; in fact, it is an unheard of complication, when pure metaphysical influence can be exerted unobstructed, because all the forces of natural mental control of every minute part, organ and function of the human system, are brought to bear, through the patient's own mind, in super-conscious action, to remove every obstruction, establish healthy action, and build new tissue with perfect atoms and healthy molecules of material.

Through the influence of mental treatment based upon a correct understanding of metaphysical principles, natural sleep is readily established, while appetite, digestion and assimilation are invariably better than under the influence of drug medication. The sensation of pain is always kept at the lowest degree possible; frequently, even in severe cases, it is entirely removed and avoided. Under favorable circumstances the ultimate of these results may be produced. They are not in any sense miraculous, but are perfectly natural results of mental action established through clear understanding of the laws of life.

It is not yet within the scope of mental action to set a broken bone of important size, which is so far displaced that mechanical appliance is necessary for support. In such event, a competent surgeon is required to properly reduce the fracture, and to splint and ligate, so that the bones cannot leave their natural position; otherwise nature has no power to repair the injury. This work is purely mechanical and absolutely necessary. In similar cases severe physical injury to tissue may require the same aid. The muscular system, however, is more directly under control of mental action, and many surprising results in changing muscular conditions are readily produced by thought influences.

The surgeon has the mechanical knowledge required to properly set the bones, cleanse, ligate, stitch, secure and make outwardly comfortable the injured parts, and to see that suitable cleansing and mechanical repairing are properly attended to until recovery, but that is the extent of his field of action. He cannot direct the placing of a single atom in reconstruction—he can only make the patient fairly comfortable and wait for Nature to do the rest.

Now the Nature which restores tissue is Universal Mind in super-conscious activity; her laws are the laws of mind and her methods are mental actions. Through his knowledge of these methods and laws, so far as yet acquired, the rightly educated metaphysician readily reaches the case, removes obstructions, and assists in establishing natural action. No human power can do more, or do it in any better way. The only advancement possible lies in the increase of knowledge, and metaphysicians are laboring earnestly to add to the present store of information.

Nature's ways are the ways of life, health, strength, comfort and happiness. The active force of Nature is the Universal Mind, which is always alive and always strong in the activity of Spirit. Spiritual Intelligence is the active principle of every individual mind.

The Soul of the universe is one magnificent unit of essential principle. The Life of the universe is one grand whole of active law. By exercise of the divine faculty of intelligent comprehension, each individual may share all the innate good of both these universal realities.

To some it seems easier to accept the opinions of others than to directly investigate facts. Indolence fosters ignorance; ignorance begets superstition; superstition stultifies every comprehensive faculty, and man thereby becomes a mere machine, moving only when some outer agency works the treadle. In this position he is a fit subject for the miracle theory, which seems little better than an attempt to evade the fact that nature is continually pushing fresh facts and deeper truths before the human intellect for recognition. These facts must be freely investigated by each individual or he is sure to be overwhelmed by the continual accumulation of evidences of the infinite and eternal activities of the universe.

The elation of self-satisfied opinion proves a stumbling-block to many an otherwise brilliant intellect, and the circle of self-limitation, which some draw in space, temporarily closes the door of the soul to the most limpid truths of the universe. No greater mistake than this could possibly be made.

There is no one so learned that he need know no more—none so wise that he cannot be advantageously instructed. There is no man whose greatness may inclose the universe, and none so powerful but that a lack of understanding of some ever-active fundamental law of his own being may trip him in the midst of his triumph. There is space beyond every boundary line, and all space is occupied by something real and true. The principle of Truth is ubiquitous.

CHAPTER IV.

THE PROGRESS OF THE AGE.

Universal Ether and Telepathy.

This nineteenth century is a period of marvelous unfoldment for the human race. Its onward movement in mechanical improvements and mathematical acquirements, is a magnificent example of the achievements which are possible to the human intellect. The limit of improvement in mechanical invention has not yet been reached, however, in any field of discovery, and soil both new and fruitful will be turned for centuries to come. Neither has the individual mind yet reached its limit of comprehension in spiritual matters: vastly greater strides in mental development are yet to be made during this century.

The extraordinary progress now being made may, perhaps, be considered as a culmination of all the enlightened acquirements of the past centuries, in preparation for a grand effulgence of illumination on the intellectual and spiritual side of human nature during the twentieth century, when progressive changes far beyond present comprehension are in store for the race. If this be doubted, we should remember that our immediate ancestors confidently declared impossible, improvements which are to-day the easy achievements of even a novice, and which any intelligent child now recognizes as established facts.

On the physical plane, this progress is perhaps best illustrated by the changes, with constant increase of power and efficiency, in methods of artificial lighting—from the dismal, smoky pine-knot of earlier centuries to the brilliant electric light of to-day. The progress made during the last three decades has developed for common use lights so many times more powerful than any dreamed of in our childhood, that even predictions of their possibility would have been derided as the vaporings of a visionary. But electricity as a medium for lighting is now an established fact, and will soon supersede all other methods of lighting, increasing in efficiency, and preparing the way to a still higher, purer and more effective light in the near future. For the end is not yet; the next step in this direction will be one in which light many times more effective will be produced without sensible combustion, and machines many times more powerful, because more simple in construction, will run without fuel, while waste, noise or danger, to any such degree as now prevails, will be considered barbarous.

One interesting feature of this subject is especially worthy of notice. Every step forward in the development of artificial lighting has been a step up and away from a considerable proportion of the gross material consumed in producing the inferior light.

The pine-knot, coarse and crude in material, burned with much smoke, shedding little light.

Next came the grease lamp in which fat was burned through a common wick; here the material used was finer than the pine-knot, yet a better and clearer light resulted from its combustion. The tallow candle is an example of this method, consuming still less crude material and giving a steadier light, while spermaceti, more refined, burns brighter than tallow.

Oil lamps, for burning fish and animal oils, came next in order, with a similar proportion of increase in power and brilliancy of the light, as the crude materiality of the medium decreases. Refinement of material gives refinement in result, with corresponding increase of effectiveness.

Following these, in natural progression, we find the various mineral oils, kerosene, naphtha and their numerous preparations, in which the grossness of material has largely disappeared, and light many times more brilliant results, together with the development of powerful explosive qualities.

The succeeding step is the discovery of illuminating gas which is so much finer in substance that to three of the five physical senses it is non-existent; for it can not be seen, heard or touched, yet the volume and brilliancy of its light renders insignificant all previous means of lighting.

Utilization of the light-producing power of electricity, however, proves a still greater advancement and develops a volume of light, possessing such power of penetration, brilliancy, softness and purity that we are tempted to exclaim in ecstasy—now, surely, we have reached the ultimate! But there is need of caution lest we fasten ourselves to the same stake of limited comprehension based upon sense-evidence, which has held others before us in bondage. There is no ultimate within human comprehension: there is always a beyond, an above, a higher than has yet been reached; and he who would recognize the ever-broadening horizon of intelligent comprehension, must always remain with open eyes and freedom of thought, ready to perceive the first glimmer of the brighter light beyond his present vision. Reality is infinite; the only existing limit is that of individual comprehension, and this is susceptible of continuous expansion. All permanent activity is in ever-widening circles, and the action of every circle is in the endless progression of a continuous expansion, which necessitates perpetual development. This is real life.

All progress in the production of artificial light has been up from and out of materiality, and away from sense-evidence, until now we have a light that is immeasurably greater than any other, produced apparently from a physical element that cannot be directly recognized by the exercise of any of the five physical senses. Always—the greatest degree of power is generated from the smallest proportion of crude material. Why?

If molecular matter, which appeals to the physical senses, is the only reality of the universe, or even more real than its other components, then why is it not a fact that the more material the medium for combustion, the more powerful and better the light produced? Can it be that the less reality there is employed the more real will be the result obtained? Or, must we consider light and power unreal?

The indisputable fact that power increases in inverse ratio to the grossness of the material, in every power-producing medium, gives rise to the suggestion which has been followed out and proved true,—that power does not exist in matter itself but that it subsists in Intelligence, which is the foundation of real substance, and a perpetually active force of the universal Spirit Nature, shared by every individual in proportion to his intelligent realization of its qualities.

The less we trust the evidence of the physical senses, the less we place dependence upon molecular matter, the more receptive we become to the real force of Spiritual Essence which pervades all space, and the more actual power we realize. This axiom has been demonstrated by every important mechanical advancement made in any of the sciences and in every power-producing medium, from the muscular exertion of the animal up through all grades of molecular action in water, air and steam to that marvelous force, electricity, which in the winking of an eye, bores through solid masonry or through metal plates without visible implement or evident means.

Steam also is invisible; and, if the inside of a steam-chest be examined without admitting atmosphere, at the time when the greatest amount of power is concentrated within, an empty chamber is all the eye reports. On mingling with the atmosphere, steam re-assumes its coarser form, again becoming visible as vapor, but in the change its power as steam is lost. Water must become invisible in order that the greater power, Steam, may be developed from it. So material element must become intangible that the greatest of physical powers may be demonstrated through electrical action.

Electricity is the lowest degree of the molecular motion of the universal element now recognized as Ether, an infinitely fine and volatile fluid which pervades all the space of the material Universe, exactly as the atmosphere permeates all parts of this earth.

In some form or other all the fundamental elements of the earth are presented in every substance. All possible chemical *combinations* of elements are not embodied in any separate object, but the fundamentals are invariably present in some form. Each coarser material is entirely permeated by particles of the element next finer in constitution.

An object which seems to be solid, without either particles or interstices, when examined under the microscope proves to be all particles and interstices, without real solidity or continuous substance.

These interstices may be permeated by any element composed of finer particles. They usually are filled with several finer elements, each within the other.

A piece of granite appears solid, while in fact it is exceedingly porous. Sufficient pressure will crowd it into smaller limits and force water from its pores. This is equally true of every solid and liquid constituent of the earth.

The water which fills the pores of the stone is composed of particles, and the spaces between these are occupied with still finer elements of a gaseous nature. In this manner air permeates water, the two varying in proportion according to temperature and local conditions.

The constituents of the earth are described as solids, liquids and gases. Each appears in some degree less solid than the next coarser in construction. Each is composed of particles separated by spaces which are filled with finer elements. There is, therefore, no empty space, in the literal meaning of the term; because, be the space ever so small, there is some element so small, so fine in construction, as to find an abiding place within its chamber. Neither is there in matter any absolutely solid substance. Each element is saturated with every finer substance, all uniting in one volatile fluid which perpetually changes, never becoming actually fixed in either position or condition. All seeming solidity is an illusion of the physical senses.

For every material substance there are elements finer in construction, the particles of which enter its interstices, forcing molecules further apart, until that element ceases to exist as an aggregation of particles or a molecular mass, whereupon it vanishes from sight.

No material substance is sufficiently solid to escape this universal interaction which is constantly taking place in all bodies and in all elements.

The diamond is the hardest substance in common use; yet, "heated in oxygen gas, it burns to pure carbonic acid, which at ordinary pressure and temperature is a colorless, transparent fluid." This change becomes possible only through the power of the finer molecules of oxygen gas to enter the interstices and force apart the particles of carbon which constitute the diamond.

A finer may always be found within the coarser— not necessarily embodied in its elemental construction, but occupying the spaces not occupied by the other. The finer element passes unobstructed through the coarser substance, as persons pass from room to room of a building. A communication may be passed through the building, either by a messenger, or by voice transmitted in atmospheric vibrations. In a corresponding manner, communication may be established between intelligent beings through every physical element, by means of the finer vibrations. Knowledge of the nature of that element is the only requirement. Its modes of undulation and vibration are the physical means of communication.

The recognized solids of the earth are permeated with liquids, of which water is the principal constituent. All liquids are permeated by air, and by gases which are of still finer construction, and gases are pervaded by finer bodies of their own nature.

Higher chemical experiments show that nothing in the material world stands separate, independent and alone. This proves a unity of construction, even in the most changeable planet of the universe. The principle of Unity therein expressed makes every portion of the universe an integral part of the whole, therefore each part bears some relation to every other part. When this relation is understood, power to deal with related elements is developed, which makes the operator master of the situation.

This fact is forcibly demonstrated in chemistry, the simplest principles of which reveal a power over the elements which astonishes the novice.

Through the principle of Unity expressed in the permeating and intermingling of all the elements of the earth, the intelligent mind gains access to every part of the planet, unobstructed by element, action or distance. The water with which the stone is saturated permits transmission through its body of vibrations more delicate than could possibly be carried by the mass of the stone itself. The air contained in a body of water makes undulations possible which could not exist in drops devoid of air. Certain finer forces which pervade the atmosphere render simple and easy the transmission of light in vibrations too infinitely fine to travel by means of particles or molecules of atmosphere alone.

Of all the constituents of the earth the atmosphere seems the most nearly universal, for it not only surrounds the globe, extending many miles into space, but it pervades all the space in and between the particles of every object and of every element.

Pure atmosphere is beyond the reach of the senses; no image of atmosphere can be impressed upon the retina of the eye. Objects are seen to move in the wind, therefore we infer that air is in motion, but the wind cannot be seen. Neither does atmosphere appeal directly to the sense of hearing; the vibrations of substances coarser than the atmosphere are transmitted through it and registered upon the drum of the ear, but air itself is not recognized by hearing. Nor does it appeal to smell, taste or touch in direct action. Varying degrees of the density and proportion of its gases are recognized in heat and cold, but these are only physical changes in its elemental composition. Yet, though it is not directly perceivable through sense-action, the atmosphere is a known constituent of the earth, which takes constant and active part in the development and continuance of the planet, as well as of every living thing in it.

Ether is even more pervasive in character and activity than atmosphere, and though further beyond the reach of sense-action, still its existence can be proved in a number of ways as indisputable as those by which the presence of the atmosphere is known. Its modes of activity also may be intelligently studied. Ether is the principal element of all universal objectivity, and the fundamental element of material composition—Matter itself. Ether unites all bodies of the universe in one entire whole of materiality.

This universal element permeates everything material, filling all interstices, even between the atoms of every molecule, however tiny in size or intricate in construction. As the heavings of an earthquake are at once transmitted in vibrations of the coarser rock-strata of the earth, and heavings of the ledge of rock are thence conveyed in undulations through the water, while the beating of the waves and rushing of the waters might be still further transmitted through atmospheric vibrations, and then in turn throb through the Ether itself to stir the inner recesses of the senses; so this infinitely fine, volatile and elastic element transmits, in most delicate rhythm, the finest and most subtle movements engendered by the activity of thought in the individual mind, throughout the extent of the ethereal fluid. And as a vibration established at one end of a telegraphic cable is also felt and understood all along the line and as far as the metallic medium extends, so the rhythmic movements established in the ethereal fluid of the universe will go where directed, and may be understood by that intelligence which receives the communication.

This fact is not only the seeming mystery, but on the material plane it is the manifestation of the Law of Thought-transference, which is now attracting the attention of the best thinkers in the civilized world. Its scientific name is Telepathy.

Telepathy is a Universal Law, just as simple in operation and as easy to comprehend as those laws with which we are more familiar; but being a comparatively new idea to modern thinkers it is not so well understood. This universal Ether is the medium through which communication on the material plane always has been established in all physical modes of sound, sight and feeling, and it is in this almost unexplored field of action that man has within the last century begun to discover the tremendous power of electricity. When the laws which govern Ether are better understood, electricity will be comparatively a plaything.

The power of conscious thought is not limited in action even to the ethereal plane of activity, but reaches beyond to higher planes where those powers prevail which govern all material movement.

In and through, between and around every atom of the Universal Ether, filling all so-called space in the entire Universe of Universes, is yet another element, as much finer in character, in degree and in action than the Ether itself, as this element is finer than the rock-strata of the earth; so fine in substance and so pure in character that it cannot be measured with the instruments or comprehended by the rules which are employed in even the finest material measurements. This is the element of Spiritual Substance: Intelligence itself—the active principle of the entire Universe—the Soul of the Ethereal Universe. Conscious Thought is the only Instrument which can be employed in its manifestation. With this keen instrument, trained to work in the real laws of pure Intelligence, the human soul breaks the fetters of sensation and soars unrestrained to fields of reality, where Principles and their resulting laws are the only objects of perception.

Thought is wholly immaterial, yet a thousand times more subtle, rapid, clear and powerful in action than the highest material element or agency; for Thought is a Spiritual Activity, and when rightly controlled through knowledge of its laws, it is an agency of, as nearly as may be, unlimited resources.

Without the power of conscious Thought the most brilliant electric light would be but Stygian darkness to any individual, and atomic vibrations would have no existence.

Consciousness is a living reality. Divine Consciousness, in active thought, eternally creates the Universe—an actual entity of spiritual substance, divine in nature and eternal in duration. Physical things are objective projections of particular phases of this Thought-activity, and the Material Universe is but the sum total of this projection of conscious thought.

If Divine Consciousness could terminate its thought the Universe would disappear, because the Principles and Qualities of things would have ceased to be.

Conscious, intelligent comprehension of Principle illumines every depth and banishes every doubt.

CHAPTER V.

INTELLIGENCE AND SENSATION.

The Office of the Senses.

SPIRITUAL Intelligence is the active force of the Universe. It is projected in Thought-activity, reflected in the atomic action of Ether, inverted in the molecular dispersion of Gases, and fully materialized in crude matter recognizable through sense-evidence.

The vital activity of every individual is a living, spiritual essence of real Being—an element of pure intelligence, capable of thinking and knowing. Through certain modes of reflected action, the physical proceeds from, and is governed by, spiritual activities; therefore, knowledge of the spiritual side of human nature gives a comprehensive understanding of the physical also, while knowledge based entirely upon physical evidence is confined to that plane alone for action, and gives information only by self-limited sense-evidence.

The action of the physical senses is gauged entirely for the material plane of life and they report only the physical phenomena which they are fitted to measure, leaving the investigator destitute of understanding of that real part of all nature which is above and beyond their realm, and out of reach of their powers.

The evidence of the physical senses is relative only, and cannot be relied upon for accurate report on any subject; their natural office is to report the presence of the manifold forms of physical phenomena which successively result from the varieties of motion prevalent among universal activities. Beyond this they are inoperative.

No one can think solely through exercise of any of the five senses. With these instruments evidence of the presence of physical things can be gained in varying degrees of intensity, but Ideas pass unrecognized. Power to think intelligently on a given subject depends upon recognition of the principles involved in the Ideas upon which that subject is founded. Even the power to "sense" the presence of an object depends upon some degree of such recognition; because sensation depends upon Consciousness and the activities of consciousness are expressed through thought. Without comprehension of Principles there can be no definite thought-action, and without thought there is no sensation. Without sensation the object would pass unrecognized.

Sensation means recognition of the presence of material objects; its common name is Feeling. On the physical plane the sense of Feeling has five outward modes of action, namely: Hearing—which is feeling the vibrations of the atmosphere; Seeing—which is feeling the ethereal vibrations of light; Smelling and Tasting—which are modes of feeling the molecular vibrations spoken of as flavors and odors; and Touching, commonly recognized as Feeling, which is a consciousness of resistance of objects or elements.

While exercising sense faculties, physical phenomena are recognized. In right process of thought it is known that these appear before us only because of the existence of the eternal Principles of Reality, which subsist back of all phenomena. This knowledge enables man to reason calmly back from physical phenomena to the underlying metaphysical facts, where he gains a substantial foothold in the understanding of principles which are above sensations. Without these principles, always subsisting in the spiritual realm, there could not possibly be any sensation of any kind, degree or quality. It is because of the absolute and perpetual necessity for the presence of these Subsisting Principles, that a knowledge of them becomes essential to progress.

Principles underlie all Objective Things;—" Qualities are the only real parts of things." If an object lose its qualities, only a lifeless shell remains, which must speedily disintegrate; because each quality is a direct expression of the Principle on which that thing was constructed. Mathematical character is the *form* of its existence, while the active principle of the object is the *spirit* of its being. Without quality, principle and character, an object can have neither being nor existence and must instantly cease to appear.

No mathematical principle is involved in any act of direct sensation; therefore, no mathematical conclusion can be arrived at through the senses alone.

"The physical senses were never intended to be used as Philosophical instruments. Their office is solely to report the presence of objective things." Subjective Principles and Ideas are above their plane of action and cannot be defined by them. Accurate description of qualifications and characteristics, as well as correct measurement of the objects themselves, involves a just exercise of the higher faculty, Reason, which, because it is a faculty of the spiritual Intelligence, can appreciate qualities as well as sizes, thus accurately determining the facts of existence embodied in any object. This, the external senses cannot do; therefore, evidence given by them invariably falls short of necessary data for accurate information, and should not be trusted as means to a final conclusion.

The faculty of vision, if accurately tested, will illustrate this shortcoming. The remark is frequently heard, "What I see I can believe"; and the average person is quite indignant if doubt of his ability to see things as they are is expressed; yet it is an indisputable fact that we never see anything as it really is in the material universe; neither do any two persons see the same thing exactly alike. You do not know how another person sees an object; you only know how it appears to you—that is, you know your interpretation of your own Vision, but not any other person's interpretation of his Vision. Color, form, dimension, distance, solidity—all vary in some degree with every observer; sometimes radical differences occur.

A cambric needle appears to be a tiny bit of very smooth and highly polished steel, with an absolute point of no dimensions. The sense of feeling corroborates the evidence of sight, because the needle feels absolutely smooth, and the sharpness of a point is plainly felt and seems to be present; but put the needle under a microscope and the illusion vanishes. The seeming point is revealed as a clumsy, blunt or ragged end, with no suggestion of sharpness; the seemingly bright, polished surface is seen to be rough and lustreless. There is nothing present to even suggest what the eye *seemed* to see before the microscope disclosed the truth.

In which instance is vision to be regarded as correct? Is the piece of steel as vision reports it, or as the microscope shows it to be? Is it the office of the microscope to change right impressions of things to those which are wrong? Is it not, rather, to correct the coarseness of natural vision and to bring objects before the understanding in a degree nearer to their true state? Do the lenses of the microscope enlarge the object? Do they not, rather, multiply the power of vision to the extent that more of the real nature of the object is recognized?

The fact is, the microscope enables the observer to come in closer contact with the true qualities of the object and to reason better concerning what is seen, and thus the inference drawn from sense-evidence becomes more accurate.

In the needle, the qualities of sharpness, smoothness and lustre are not present as realities of the molecular construction of the article, but as illusions of the sense of sight. This illusion exists because of inability to see the particles composing the object, the eye as an instrument being proportionately so coarse that it cannot come in effective contact with them. Vision acute enough to enable one to see the atoms comprising the steel would render the observer powerless, so far as vision is concerned, to recognize the needle itself, or to know its usefulness.

Already the Microscope has opened the door to an entirely new world, of the most marvelous construction, too fine to be apprehended through external sense; but for the discovery of this mathematical instrument it would still remain unrecognized. If the power of lenses be increased, there will be discovered yet other and more marvelous worlds of life-activities on every hand, in the midst of what now *seems* to be the entire creation.

There may be brought forward by any thinker various illustrations similar in character in regard to the power and scope of the senses, which prove them instruments incapable of estimating measurements accurately.

When qualities are observed through the senses, they are interpreted relative to other qualities, similar in character. Objects are either large or small, long or short, wide or narrow, hard or soft, heavy or light; in temperature, hot or cold; in color,.light or dark; in sensation, acute or dull: and qualities are either good or bad, even right or wrong, according to comparison with other objects or qualities. Neither these nor any real characteristics of objects can be definitely determined by sense-power.

The evidence of the senses is susceptible of correction by man himself; therefore, sense-power is not man's highest power, because the most powerful cannot be over-powered—the highest cannot be corrected.

Most people suppose they believe the evidence of their senses, yet every intelligent thinker is constantly reasoning beyond their pale. The intelligent mechanic never trusts sense-evidence exclusively, but has an instrument by which to determine every measurement. Frequently, as in the case of some finely constructed astronomical instruments, a second instrument is required to register and interpret the information given through the first, for which purpose the senses are known to be inadequate.

In some problems mathematical calculation and processes of reasoning are necessary in order to arrive at a correct interpretation of measurements. In fact, no true mathematician ever trusts his senses further than to read the coarsest of characters and to furnish crude material with which to begin investigation; any degree of confidence beyond this leads to erroneous conclusions and corresponding disaster.

Sensation reports the presence of a phenomenon. What it really is; what are its dimensions, its character, its qualities; what principles are involved in its formation, what is its nature, object and scope — all these are entirely beyond the power of sensation to determine, and no accurate information whatever in regard to them can be gained by direct action of the senses. Every point of description is a matter of inference drawn by the observer; and wrong inference is the result of faulty reasoning with regard to the appearance. Through accurate reasoning wrong evidence may be corrected and the truth learned concerning that object.

This is a vital point in considering the question of the nature and cause of sickness, because the reported evidence of the sense of feeling is involved in every case. This sense is no more reliable than any of the others; its evidence requires the equalizing influence of reason, in order that the real condition underlying the feeling, may be correctly interpreted.

Feeling gives evidence only with regard to external molecular vibrations. The real character of the sickness depends upon inner activities beyond the scope of this sense; therefore, to trust its evidence absolutely would be, in every instance, to draw erroneous conclusions which in treatment might lead to disastrous results.

Through the physical senses alone no one can comprehend a mathematical principle or solve even the simplest problem; senses deal with externals only, while some faculty within the individual goes deeper, higher, and perceives the principles underneath the grouping of objects.

Comprehensive understanding of Principle is a faculty which every sane human being possesses; animals lack this, though they have all the physical sense-faculties, sometimes even to a greater degree of acuteness than man. In the dog or in the weasel the sense of smell is more acute than in man. The eagle has power to gaze on the midday sun. Many varieties of insects and animals see both by night and by day; thus what we call darkness becomes non-existent for them.

Animals, also, have power to think—to reason about things and objects on the plane of their own life, to recognize facts of experience and results of action, with, in some instances, marked exercise of memory; yet animals have not developed the faculty of intelligent comprehension of Principle. This is a spiritual faculty of divine origin belonging to the higher and purer side of human nature, above the animal intelligence and beyond the sense-plane, but capable of being understood and intelligently employed for a purpose. Knowledge acquired through conscious exercise of this natural faculty, conveys power for action which is unattainable by the development of the physical, the sensuous, or even the intellectual, alone. The innate good of power thus generated can be recognized only through direct comprehension of principles.

Spiritual faculties can be exercised only through pure motive and for a good purpose; because they are absolutely pure in nature, and purity can never defile. The intellect, when perverted by self-desire on the sense-plane, may start a wrong action, and state a false premise; but spiritual understanding can neither make the statement nor believe it to be true. Spiritual comprehension either takes no part in the transaction, as when an error is innocently committed, or, through the inspired voice of conscience, protests against the outrage when a wrong act is decided upon for a willful purpose. The native purity of spiritual Principle remains unchanged, however, and eventually compels the righting of each wrongful act.

The natural retribution of outraged Principle begins to take effect within the mind of him who fails to follow the Principles comprehended, as soon as the act is committed; the corresponding result is only a matter of time unless the right action is speedily re-established. The slowness of the change or process may blind one's eyes for a while, but Principle cannot be permanently transgressed: it is the eternal activity of the universe and eventually must be complied with by every one. Failure to comply with Principle, for any reason whatever, either intentional or accidental, is existence, for the time of transgression, outside the perpetual harmony of its native purity. On the earth-plane, sorrow, sickness and untimely death follow continuance of erroneous action, to all classes alike. Neither saint nor sinner can claim favor of the law.

Opinion is equally inoperative here, as in the working of any mathematical problem—nothing short of complete recognition of the Principle involved, and absolute compliance with it, can solve any problem. But with this degree of compliance the right solution is inevitable.

The facts of Absolute Truth are unconditioned.

CHAPTER VI.

MENTAL ACTION.

The Process of Thought.

THE Theory of Metaphysical Healing presents three distinct statements:

(a) Mind antedates and is superior to body.

(b) Each mind governs its own body through definite laws of mental action.

(c) By certain erroneous lines of thought conditions of disease are generated, which may be removed, and health restored, by establishing different modes of action.

These statements differ somewhat from those generally entertained in regard to the nature, the probable causes and possible cures of sickness, and in order to understand them fully it will be necessary to examine the thinking process of mind.

What is the process of Thought? How does Mind think? These are questions which invariably arise at the outset of investigation of this subject. They are not difficult to answer, if certain facts concerning thought are taken into consideration.

Thought is mental action. The intelligent individual thinks. Conscious activity of the mental faculties results in the formation of a thought-image in mind; the individual has intelligently conceived something—that *something* is an Idea.

Ideas are entities composed of spiritual substance—spiritual things. In substance, they are real; in activity, living; in endurance, eternal. Each is a permanent reality. Living Principle is the essence of every true Idea.

Thought is the process of forming, among the conscious activities of mind, a mental image or picture of the Idea which at that moment is the object of consciousness. There is no other method or means of thought—no different thought-activity. The mental process of conscious thought consists in clearly seeing and intelligently understanding the form, shape, size, color, qualities and other characteristics of ideas which already exist in universal mind, on the spiritual plane of Being. The detail of the process is mental; but the final intelligent comprehension is a spiritual act of high degree, in which physical sense takes no part.

A true Thought is an Idea individually recognized. Ideas are founded upon fundamental principles of truth. To become conscious of a real Idea is to recognize a fundamental truth—a permanent principle of the universe.

When the character and quality of an Idea are fully recognized, a picture of that Idea is instantaneously impressed upon the living substance of mind. Conscious recognition of the Idea, and impression of the picture, are simultaneous in action. The Idea is a permanent, unchanging reality, perfect in every detail. The mental picture will correspond exactly to the interpretation of the Idea. It may be either perfect or imperfect, complete or incomplete, correct or incorrect, true or false, according to the quality of the thought. Imperfection in the thought, however, does not change the nature of the Idea—it affects only the thinker, in his relation to that Idea.

Through exercise of true thought the real Idea is recognized in its native purity and perfection. In this process the thinker, acting through pure intelligence, mounts upward to the spiritual plane and recognizes truth itself. Through incorrect thought one sees darkly, interprets imperfectly, and forms a temporary picture correspondingly inaccurate, based upon an appearance which does not correspond to any real Idea. Yielding to the illusions of sense, man withdraws from the uplifting influence of intelligence and retrogrades to the material plane where mere appearances seem real and illusions becloud the intellect.

This form of thought possesses no principle or real quality; has therefore no permanence and cannot endure. It is a seeming, which passes away—a falsity, an illusion. It seems to possess power, but the seeming exists on the sense-plane only, and always bears relation to some object of sense-recognition. It is a sensation rather than a thought.

In either act of thought, mind forms a picture which is a copy of its own comprehension of the subject. Clearness in the picture depends upon the purity with which the qualities of the Idea are recognized.

Words do not necessarily bear direct relation either to Ideas or to Thoughts; at best they are imperfect, incomplete, only crude symbols of thoughts, and frequently inadequate to express the Idea conceived.

Mind recognizes Ideas, thinks about them by forming mental pictures, and explains what it thinks in words. To think, therefore, is to recognize an **Idea**; and to think rightly is to form in mind a correct picture of the Idea, intelligently comprehending all its subjective details. If the Idea is not consciously recognized, no mental picture is formed; in which case there can be no mental action, no thought on that subject, and no information gained.

True knowledge cannot be acquired in conscious thought on the plane of this life, without the purely mental act of picturing in mind the qualifications of some real, subjective Idea; this act can not take place without spiritual comprehension of the principles involved in that Idea.

To one familiar with the English language the sound of the word *apple* instantly arouses in mind a more or less complete and perfect picture of that fruit. Each mind, however, adds to its first impression of the Idea the detailed characteristics of size, color, flavor, etc., with which previous experience in conscious recognition of apples has made it familiar. If several persons hear the word *apple*, each, perhaps, sees in mind somewhat different characteristics of the Idea:—to one, the apple seems red, to another yellow, while still another thinks of it as variegated in color, large or small, sweet or sour, according to his previous conceptions. Though the correct idea, *apple*, be aroused in the mind of each by hearing the same sound, yet each mind in its own thinking process is at work supplying with lightning rapidity those qualifications which go to make up some special kind of apple. This detailed thought-process does not take place, however, unless the Idea is aroused in consciousness, and a mental picture of the idea enters the activity of that mind. If no Idea is comprehended no picture is seen, and no conscious thought occurs.

Suppose the word *apple* to be spoken for the first time in the hearing of one unacquainted with the English language. It makes no conscious impression upon his mind; therefore, it arouses no conscious thought with reference to any object. He does not recognize the word as associated with any Idea. To him it is not even a word, but only a meaningless disturbance of atmospheric vibrations. No Idea is aroused in his intelligent understanding by the sound vibration, therefore he sees no mental picture; but speak the word which, in his native tongue, is associated with that Idea, and he will instantly proceed in conscious thought to picture the idea with every quality of which he had previously gained an understanding.

Mind thinks, both by seeing mental pictures of Ideas previously comprehended, and by consciously picturing ideas newly acquired.

True mental pictures are correct copies of ideas. If the ideas are clearly comprehended the pictures will be rightly interpreted. Ideas are seen directly through the sense of spiritual perception, and comprehended through the faculty of spiritual understanding. The physical senses are not essential to this process—indeed, they are entirely inadequate for any degree of its activity. Intelligence and Sensation are opposite in character.

Ideas are spiritual. Pictures are mental and sensations are sensuous, while objective things are physical, both in character and construction.

The process of understanding an Idea is a purely spiritual act, performed through a clear comprehension of the principles upon which that Idea is founded. Intelligence is the Instrument employed.

The process of apprehending, interpreting and imaging a correct understanding of Spiritual Ideas, is metaphysical, and the Spiritual Intellect is the active Instrument. Intellect apprehends, Reason interprets and Imagination images, or pictures in mind, the degree of intelligent comprehension of the Idea which is under examination.

Seeing mental pictures held in other minds, without conscious effort to interpret or understand on the part of the thinker, is psychical: the Imaging Faculty abnormally exercised, through inverted reflection of the original Image, is the Instrument employed in psychical action. In the process of reflection every Image is inverted; therefore, the information gained through psychical process will be misleading, unless interpreted through Intelligence by comparison with the true Idea.

The process of examining objective things is sensuous, and sensation is the instrument employed. Sensation is limited in power to examination of the coarsest of physical phenomena, and never gives accurate information concerning the qualities and character of any element. Reality is entirely beyond its pale, and never seems to have existence while the evidences of sensation are relied upon in investigation.

If the individual exercises no intellectual faculty above the sense-plane, he remains, in action, a mere animal; for even the brute creation shares with him every kind and every degree of power contained in the five senses. But if he rises a step higher, thus becoming open to the influence of pictures of better things, active in thinking minds, he gains an impetus upward, through right exercise of the Imagination, and begins to think and to reason on a higher plane, which leads to deeper understanding.

Even in psychical action he is not entirely above the animal plane, and his impulses require careful attention. Intelligent animals have the faculty of seeing mental pictures, and are susceptible to similar influence in either direction, both from their own kind and from the minds of men. The intelligent dog knows the thought of his master, and frequently acts on his suggestion without a word or any outward sign. The picture in the mind of his master is a law unto him. The average horse of good spirit knows immediately if the driver lacks self-confidence (sometimes before he is seen), and is quick to take advantage of it. Animals seldom attack one who remains firm and absolutely fearless, particularly if a thought of universal sympathy with, and appreciation of the good qualities inhering in all forms of life be extended to each in reasonable proportion.

The power of the human eye to subdue passion in the savage beast is universally recognized, though not generally understood. The human mind, acting through its thought-picture which is projected outward from the eye, in reflection of the image of thought, is the force which, with the irresistible power of spiritual intelligence, overpowers the brute impulse in the beast. If perfectly exercised through pure intelligence, it would conquer in every instance. Intelligence is greater than animal impulse, in either man or beast, and mind is more powerful than any form of matter.

If properly guarded and rightly exercised, psychic development may be a means of at least humanizing the animal tendencies in man, eventually leading him to give due attention to his higher faculties.

Metaphysical understanding leads one to cease depending on the influence of pictures reflected from the minds of others, and to think for himself— to form his own mental pictures, so far as possible, through independent, conscious thought regarding the real ideas with which he comes in contact.

Reasoning upwards from first impressions of ideas—first, by psychic help from minds that have consciously thought in advance of us, and second, through metaphysical reasoning, with regard to powers, causes and laws—we learn to form pictures of Ideas by thought-action; we receive, digest and assimilate facts with which sensation alone never can bring us face to face; we gain understanding of principles, and spiritually see real Ideas. Such growth in understanding may be attained through right exercise of the mental faculties.

Through conscious thought, by means of its imaging faculty, Mind is under the guidance and control of intelligent understanding, from which it receives its impulses.

Mind images—pictures ideas, by means of the Imagination, which, when understood in its true sense, is the most powerful instrument of the human mind. This faculty of imaging ideas is a marvelous faculty; indeed, the imagination is the most wonderful of all human instruments. It is the intelligent activity of the spiritual side of human nature, and the only faculty through which the thinker can gain pure understanding of any subject; because it is the only faculty of conscious, intellectual action, and the only instrument with which principles may be examined. It is the least understood, because least studied, being considered by superficial thinkers a distorted rather than a real faculty.

The Imagination, using the word in its true sense, is of first importance, and should be thoroughly mastered by every individual. When rightly used it will prove the most efficient instrument for analyzing the evidence of the physical senses, and deducing actual facts from the evidences presented;

then principles will be recognized and laws discovered, giving knowledge of life as it was intended to be, and as it really is, on the spiritual plane of existence, and also as it will be on the mental plane when the imaging faculty of mind is thoroughly understood. Healthy conditions and harmonious sensations are inevitable results of the acquirement of this knowledge.

Imagination is the active instrument of that invisible but real operator, the spiritual Individual who acts through understanding of principles. If not allured into wrong channels through the seemingly accurate evidence of the physical senses, it will help to rightly interpret the activities of real life as expressed in the fundamental principles of human existence on all planes — physical, mental and spiritual.

The Spiritual is a permanent plane of *real*, intelligent principle.

The Mental is a progressive plane of *actual* intellectual comprehension.

The physical is a temporary and constantly changing plane of *seeming*, material, reflection.

On the physical plane the thinker's *mental interpretations* of the spiritual facts of eternal reality are outwardly re-enacted in material copy.

The steps in the process may be classified as follows:

1. The fundamental Principles which are involved.
2. The Idea which is founded upon those principles.
3. Spiritual comprehension of the idea, including an understanding of its principles.
4. The mental Image of that particular comprehension of the idea.
5. The objective copy in Physical element of that mental image.

Spiritual Principles are the real entities of the universe. Spiritual Ideas are the developed activities of those principles. Metaphysical thought-concepts of those Ideas and Principles are the active Realities of human existence. These concepts vary in degree of accuracy according to the conscious recognition of each individual mind; therefore, human experience varies in accordance with the changing of the mental pictures formed during experience.

Intelligence recognizes spiritual activities.
Imagination pictures (images) the recognition.
Intellect interprets the picture.
Reason determines its qualities.
Thought brings all together in comprehension of the entire subject; therefore, Thought is a process

of reason through intellectual interpretation of the mental pictures reflecting from spiritual Ideas.

Thought is an active, intelligent power—Imagination its living instrument.

CHAPTER VII.

THE PHYSICAL REFLECTION OF THOUGHT.

Its Expression on the Body.

THE personal Human Body is a physical copy of the individual Mind, and in some part of its construction expresses its every thought.

Each function of individual thought has an exact correspondence in some function of the physical body, which instantly responds to every thought in its own domain. Corresponding to every mental function there is a physical organ which is its reflected counterpart.

Every thought-picture that is formed in mind is accurately registered in the corresponding part of that man's body.

Mental pictures react by direct reflection through the atoms and molecules of the ganglia, which comprise the ganglionic or sympathetic nervous system. The physical reflection will be like the mental act from which it reflects—it may be tempered somewhat by the qualities of the reflecting medium, but it never can be radically different in character.

The form, color and other characteristics of the thought-picture will strictly accord with the *qualities* of the Ideas examined, provided those ideas are rightly comprehended by the observer. Personal desires and intentions will have no weight against this law regarding all mental activity.

Both the actual Idea and the Principle back of it are eternally perfect. Concepts of the Idea and realizations of the Principle may vary from perfection down to utter failure, a mental picture being formed exactly like the concept, whether it be right or wrong. This picture registers in the physical system, reproducing its activities in the bodily action. In this manner the activities of all the organs of the body constantly change according to the variations of mental action.

The thought is the real thing—the body is a projected copy of that thing in physical element.

In sensation, only the physical is recognized; through intelligence, the thought itself is accessible.

Every individual thinks either sub-consciously or super-consciously on planes of mental activity both beneath and above that of his every-day conscious thinking about the things of this life. Such mental activity is not usually recognized, because the plane of *conscious* thought is the only distinctly apparent field of mental action. On the sub-conscious plane disease is generated by unnatural action and tissue is destroyed; on the super-conscious plane, healthy action takes place and tissue is reconstructed from natural ingredients contained in food, air and light.

The act of each mind in any degree of consciousness, is registered on its own body, in some form or other, producing a result which reflects the qualities of the mental act. The physical and the mental action will be alike, for the time being.

To thoroughly rid the system of wrong physical action, reflected from similar mental activity, it is necessary to strike at the root of the difficulty, changing the character of the action in that mind. When the harmful influence is dispelled, a corresponding change takes place in the body, by natural law, without conscious effort, and as a necessary consequence of the true relation which always exists between mind and body. The trouble then disappears and healthy activity is established in the physical system. This renews the action of the heart and other vital organs, cleansing the blood and purifying the entire system; while the individual mind working through natural, harmonious laws, on the super-conscious plane, restores the life of each molecule and builds new tissue, on the perfect model of that Individual's natural system, as originally constructed on ideas of fundamental health and wholeness.

As before stated, every mental activity results in a similar kind and quality of activity in the corresponding part of that mind's body. The mental image of that activity may also be transferred to other minds through reflection of the picture, in which event the corresponding action may be re-enacted in both mind and body of the one who thus absorbs the action from the mind which thinks it.

These are fundamental principles regarding mental action in its relation to the conditions of the human body. If once understood, they give an insight into the affairs of human experience, impossible to obtain through any amount of knowledge otherwise acquired.

When these facts are comprehended it will readily be seen that a realization of the true qualities of the fundamental idea, Harmony, must result in a mental picture conforming to harmonious activity; also, that the reflected copy of that mental action must inevitably have a harmonious tendency. If the idea be perfectly conceived, the thought will reflect in harmonious action through the nervous system, producing a natural condition in the physical body.

In harmonious activity, nature builds and retains a healthy body. If obstructions to healthy action be present they must, of course, be removed through right thought, after which the harmonious result will be inevitable; nothing can prevent it. On the other hand, if the mental picture be distorted or erroneous, with no enduring Idea for a fundamental principle, its temporary reflection on the body will also be distorted, resulting in corresponding degrees of discord. Consequently, sickness instead of health will ensue, either to that thinker or to some one in immediate mental contact who may absorb the disturbing influence through reflection of the mental Image. Many forms of disease are developed in this manner and transmitted between human beings of all ages and conditions, because of ignorance of the fundamental laws of life and of the natural course of mental action. Most epidemics are generated in this field of erroneous and unnecessary mental action.* Knowledge of certain laws renders such influence

---

*This subject is further explained in succeeding chapters in connection with the cause and cure of disease.

inoperative for any individual. and also even imparts power to relieve others.

The human body is a marvelously intricate machine; yet in every respect it is incalculably surpassed by the thinking mind, which is infinitely more intricate in constitution, more subtle in action, broader in scope, and greater in power and endurance.

The action of mind and body together may be illustrated materially by the action of a steam-boiler, and its accompanying machinery. The machine has many wheels, valves, pistons, shafts, tubes and other parts, all dependent upon and regulated in their motions by the power which proceeds from the steam-chest. They are utterly useless without the application of this power. The steam-chest, in turn, is a useless vessel without an influx of energy in the shape of compressed steam admitted to it from the boiler, where the steam is generated from water by means of heat.

If the boiler is constructed on scientific principles of exactness, is filled with pure water, and the right amount of fuel is supplied for combustion, steam is produced, generating power which, when admitted to the steam-chest in sufficient quantity, supplies the machine with energy sufficient to propel every part in harmonious action.

Suppose now that the engineer, finding the machine going at too high a rate of speed, places obstructions in the gearing and machinery to block the wheels and thus check speed. It is clear that the result will be disastrous. Or suppose that he should recognize only the machine with its objective mechanism, and, believing the steam-chest to be the motive power, should attempt to reduce the speed of the engine by direct work upon the steam-chest itself,—again he will only injure the machine. The only scientific way is to reduce the pressure of steam from the boiler, upon which the entire machine gradually slows down to a proper rate of speed without any attempt on the part of the engineer to act directly on the machine itself or on any of its parts.

The correspondence existing between the mechanism of the engine, with its power-producing forces, and the machinery of man's physical body controlled by mind, is remarkably clear. Both of the mistakes just enumerated as possible by injudicious management of the mechanical engine, are repeatedly made, under the name of Science, in attempts to control the organs and parts of the human machine by direct influence upon each part, instead of by appeal to the source of its energy—the thinking mind—where its every mode of action is established, and whence continuance or change must originate.

The elements and parts involved in the construction and operation of a steam engine are as follows:

    1. MACHINERY.
    2. STEAM-CHEST.
    3. BOILER.
    4. WATER.
    5. COMBUSTION.
    6. HEAT.
    7. STEAM.

If these words be described in terms which explain their character, each one represents a permanent Idea of especial importance in the Universe. The word cannot be adequately defined without expressing the Idea which it really represents.

The pipes, rods, wheels and other parts of the machinery constitute a machine, which represents the idea *Construction*.

In the Steam-chest, Energy is concentrated with which to propel the machine, and *Concentration* describes both its function and its character.

The Boiler is the active seat of the immediate development of Energy, and represents the intention or *Purpose* of the inventor.

Water is the *Substance* from which steam is evolved under the action of heat.

Combustion liberates the latent heat which is stored and concentrated in the fuel, thereby developing *Action*.

Heat transfers its *activity* to the water and generates steam; while the Steam confined in the Steam-chest ever pushes its way outward in all directions, in a natural effort to break its bonds and express its *energy* in action.

The elements, therefore, involved in the construction and operation of every steam engine are as follows:

Objective.		*Subjective.*
STEAM,	representing	ENERGY.
HEAT,	"	ACTIVITY.
COMBUSTION,	"	ACTION.
WATER,	"	SUBSTANCE.
BOILER,	"	PURPOSE.
STEAM-CHEST,	"	CONCENTRATION.
MACHINERY,	"	CONSTRUCTION.

The higher analogy between the two may be explained as follows:

WATER symbolizes the Spiritual Substance of Life—
Living Reality; mobile, elastic, limpid and pure; cleansing, healing, brightening and strengthening every living thing with which it comes in contact.

HEAT symbolizes the Spiritual Activity of the Universe, latent in all substance.

STEAM symbolizes Spiritual Energy, which proceeds from the activities of living Reality.

THE BOILER of the Engine, in its office and action, corresponds to Mind; because it is the instrument for developing and retaining Energy in the shape of developed activity. In its correct action the real purpose of the individual thinker is recognized.

COMBUSTION, or fire, on the material plane, symbolizes Thought-Action, which liberates the latent energy inhering in the substance of every intelligent being.

THE STEAM-CHEST, a receptacle in which is stored all the energy and power designed for use in that particular machine, has its correspondence in the Cardiac membrane of the body, which extends—an unbroken receptacle—from the Heart through all vessels of the arteries, the veins and the Lungs.

Every engine and machine has its exact counterpart in some part of the mechanism of the human body with its vital organs, and whatever is true of the mechanical machine is true also of the human body; while all the principles involved in the one are of equally vital importance to the other, and each subjective element represented in the power-producing forces of the machine is a constructive element of every mind. Without every part, every faculty and every function in perfect operation, the best result cannot be obtained, either with the vital or the mechanical machine.

Without heat, water would fail to develop steam, and without combustion there could be no heat. Without water, combustion and heat would be useless; and in the absence of a Boiler there could be no retention of force, and the energy of these elements could not be successfully applied through this particular machine. With no steam-chest, energy could not be concentrated, and in the absence of special machinery the concentrated energy could not be applied for a definite purpose. Steam is the active agency of this design, and without it no possible action can be established in that machine.

To return for a moment to the list of elements combined and activities involved in the steam engine: The Objective list is composed entirely of physical elements. Each one is material in construction, and in its present state can never leave the earth; yet, in character, each is distinctly spiritual, deriving its characteristics directly from the corresponding subjective principle.

The Subjective list is entirely spiritual, and belongs to the realm of active, conscious Reality. Each item of the list is an Idea in Universal mind, and has its being independent of materiality. It cannot be manifested in sensation, except through some material construction embodying its principles. But the objective representation is not the same real entity that the subjective principle is. The subjective can continue to be, independent of the existence of the objective, while the objective can have no existence apart from the subjective.

Steam illustrates Energy. Now, Energy is an infinite and eternal reality, always present in the Universe and susceptible at all times of demonstration in countless ways. Steam is but one of the existing modes of expression of the inherent power of spiritual energy. If Energy were not present in the Universe the power of Steam would never have been developed; for Steam is only the Energy that is latent in water, escaping from temporary restraint, and displaying the natural freedom of its real nature. Remove energy from steam, and its seeming qualities vanish, while the element instantly ceases to exist in that form.

By the same analogy, if the idea Substance was not present in universal mind, the element

Water would have no appearance on this or on any other planet. Substance is the life of every earthly element, uniting and holding together all its particles. If all the water of the earth were destroyed, substance would still inhere in every remaining thing. The Idea *Substance* is an ever present reality, which can neither cease to be, diminish, nor change.

Activity is ever present in each atom of every element. Without this eternal entity—a spiritual Idea, possessed of eternal life — even the atom would cease to hold its form, and would vanish. If there were no Activity there could be neither Combustion nor Heat; these constitute the body, while eternal activity is the spirit of their life. If there were no conscious Idea of a *Purpose*, a steam-boiler never could have been invented, as the boiler only expresses the purpose for which it exists—namely, to develop and retain for use the energy which exists in Water, but which is useless while seemingly confined within those narrow bounds. The Individual mind derives its idea of a Purpose from Universal Mind, where it subsists as an eternal entity of divine reality.

If the conscious Idea of Concentration were not present in universal mind, the steam-chest never would have been conceived by man; and without

Purpose, concentrated for action, the machine would have no existence.

The Life of each Objective element inheres in the essence of its corresponding Subjective element; the substance endures, while its reflected expression constantly changes. The subjective or real is spiritual; its first reflection in the mind of man is mental action.

The Material body belongs entirely in the objective realm, and is governed by the laws which relate to objective things. Under the guiding influence of mind, intelligently exercised through conscious thought, it can be perfectly controlled in accordance with Nature's universal laws of life.

In pure action, Mind is entirely subjective, and has its field of action on the spiritual plane, dealing directly with subjective elements. The thought-actions of mind transfer to and control molecular action in every part of the body, through the Mental Image of the Idea with which mind deals; for the thought-action forms a physical copy of the mental image of that idea.

In this action we may recognize a physical reflection of thought.

CHAPTER VIII.

THE MENTAL ORIGIN OF DISEASE.

Thought Images.

Can mind cause Disease? Is it possible for an act of mind without exterior physical means to produce an actual case of Sickness?

In various forms of expression this question is seriously agitating the minds of several millions of intelligent thinkers, whose attention has in one way or another been called to the statements made by the schools of Mental Healing that disease is both caused and cured by mental means.

The sentiment commonly expressed on first meeting with the idea is, that sickness is Disease, and that Disease is a physical thing possessing independent power for harm.

It is frequently stated with the utmost assurance that mind has nothing to do with Disease, except that, perhaps, the sickness may have reacted somewhat upon the mind, and that if the disease be removed by physical means the normal condition of mind will thereby be restored. One of the commonest statements heard is, "Mental treatment may answer very well for the hysterical and those of doubtful intelligence who imagine sickness but are not diseased. My sickness, however, is not imaginary; it is a genuine disease with which mind has no connection—such cases require medicine which can be swallowed, or physical treatment. Mind can neither cause nor cure physical disease."

These and kindred opinions seem to rest on a foundation of knowledge and common experience, yet every such thought is erroneous, and entertained only because the question of disease and its active cause has been viewed from but one side, while conclusions have been based upon the evidence of the physical senses, without investigation of the real activities of human nature.

Although in many cases the disease to be dealt with is a physical condition more or less clearly apparent to the senses, yet it is never absolutely certain that it is physical in every part of its nature; neither is there adequate evidence that it originated from a physical cause alone. In fact, such conclusion can only be reached through undemonstrated opinion, as the most cursory investigation of prevailing mental conditions presents numerous points of evidence that some degree of corresponding mental action in a definite direction takes place on the mental plane previous to the development of any diseased condition in Individual, Family, Community or Race.

The further honest investigation of this subject is carried, the more overwhelming becomes the accumulated evidence that disease originates in previously established mental action, which works itself out through the vital organs of the physical system, unrecognized except as the physical sensations resulting from the mental disturbances are observed. This is now a thoroughly established fact, and only those who refuse to investigate can continue to doubt the statement.

Three principal degrees of disease are now recognized. First, those conditions of the material body in which physical change of tissue has occurred in organic structure because of the continued presence of some definite unhealthy action. This form is recognized as Organic Disease, or Lesion, and is usually considered the most serious form of sickness. It is commonly supposed to bear no relation whatever to mental activity, but to be itself a physical thing, with definite power for harmful action. Such a conclusion postulates intelligence of disease, and makes it logically necessary to consider it an animal possessed of some degree of will and determination. These faculties are purely mental; therefore the animal must possess mind as well as body—the mind of a microbe instead of that of a man, but mind, nevertheless, else it would be devoid of power to plan and execute.

The human mind includes all faculties of the entire animal kingdom, combined with the higher activities of logical reasoning and intellectual comprehension of principles; therefore it possesses powers of intelligence immeasurably greater than those of any microbe, and so should readily overthrow any animal action or plan for action on the field of the human body. The one necessary condition is an adequate understanding of the laws involved.

Next in order, in the classification of diseases, comes that class of disturbances of the physical system, in which, though no physical lesion or change of structure can be discovered, yet the patient is afflicted with weakness, lack of endurance, and excitability, together with various tendencies recognized as nervous or neurotic, and classed either as diseases or functional disturbances. These, also, are generally considered actual physical diseases, affecting only the nervous system. They are usually classed under the head of neurosis or neurasthenia, and are known as neurasthetic conditions. Prominent physicians recognize that the mind probably has much to do with developing this form of disease, but usually they are unable to satisfactorily explain the mode of development, and hence are practically powerless to remove the troublesome symptoms by medication, though they study and work with great patience, confidence and hope.

In the third class of recognized diseases, marked symptoms of distress appear, without any physical lesion of tissue or definite nervous derangement that can be mechanically discovered; yet the patient evidently suffers and seems unable to control action. These cases are considered purely nervous and are frequently classed as diseases of the Imagination. It is admitted that they may originate in mind, because of a distorted imagination. It is also admitted that mental treatment may have some effect upon this class of patients, because it is supposed that nothing is the matter with them. This last opinion is a commom error, based upon misunderstanding of the case.

Almost countless names have been attached to the manifold forms of disease, but all are modes of wrong molecular action and each one comes under the head of one or the other of the three previously mentioned degrees of disorder. Distinctly named, these are:

1. Organic disease: Lesion of physical tissue developed by continued disturbance of some organ or part.

2. Nervous disorder: Disturbance of the circulation of nerve fluids, either organic or functional.

3. Hysterical, imaginary and unreal: Commonly supposed to be unnecessary and susceptible to personal control by the sufferer.

Investigation of mental action in its relation to the physical substructure discloses the fact that the three classes of disease, Organic, Neurotic and Hysterical, are closely associated in what is really one class, with three degrees of action. Also, that each lower degree prepares the way for, leads to, and finally, if permitted to continue in operation, develops to the succeeding degree in due time, under favoring conditions and circumstances. This development is not, as some suppose, from physical to mental, but *vice versa*, the original mental action eventually leading to a physical condition corresponding to its mental cause. In general observation, only the physical side is seen; consequently, the mental action that has previously been in operation is not detected; nevertheless it is an active factor in life, and has produced the physical condition.

Beginning with external evidence and tracing back for an adequate cause, the fact is disclosed that in a given case of organic disease there first existed a nervous or functional disturbance with that part of the structure, before the lesion of tissue, described by the particular form of disease became established. This nervous disturbance sometimes develops so rapidly and in so subtle a manner as not to attract attention until the organic degree is reached; but whether of long or short duration, if followed patiently and intelligently, it can invariably be traced back, through all the stages of nervousness, from the extreme symptoms bordering on the organic, perhaps through many degrees of action, to the first nervous tendencies, so slight as scarcely to be perceptible—then back still further, to some element of mental distress established before the first faint nervous tracings of the symptoms began. If this original mental action had not taken place the organic disease would never have developed.

While mental agitation continues, nervous agitation gradually, though perhaps imperceptibly, increases. It first exists in mind, sometimes developing to hysteria or melancholia, even to insanity. Prolonged disturbance of nervous circulation develops nerve exhaustion, spinal irritation and general nervous weakness. This eventually leads to disturbance of those vital organs which are the most closely associated with the nervous system, as *e. g.*, of the heart and blood vessels, producing a fever; of the digestive organs, resulting in dyspepsia; and so on through the entire system. Every organ, muscle, artery, nerve and function is under absolute control of the thinking mind which is its living intelligence. This control is exerted entirely by mind acting through the nervous system.

Next to the sympathetic system of ganglionic nerves, is the cerebro-spinal nervous system, which includes all the larger nerves and systems of nerves, supplying circulation to the principal vital organs and to the organs of sense. Following this there is a distinct system of arteries and veins; a system of vital organs; a muscular system, and a bony substructure, all of which systems unite to form one physical body. Each organ and every part of this physical structure is under the intelligent control of the thinking mind, through thought exercised on the various planes of consciousness and reflected in the mechanism of the nervous system.

The sympathetic nervous system corresponds more nearly than any other to the structure of the mental mechanism. It definitely registers every intelligent thought-activity, and faithfully reproduces every thought-picture formed in mind.

Every mental act is physically registered, either sub-consciously or super-consciously — first, directly on the brain, which is the centre of the molecular action in the nervous system; then, through the circulation of nerve fluid in all branches of both nervous systems, on the vital organs, and, in turn, by means of the circulation of the blood, in and through every part of the material body, internal and external. In this way mind, through wrong action, becomes responsible for every abnormal action in the physical system.

When clearly comprehended, the principle of the physical reflection of thought explains the numerous sicknesses of those children who are too young to think harm for themselves, yet who have mental mechanisms that register surrounding influences, frequently in the minutest detail. The modes of action expressed in those influences are afterwards re-enacted in the physical system, developing various corresponding diseases. The anxious thought of the mother, nurse or doctor, for the child, reflects to, is absorbed by and re-enacted in the little one's mental mechanism. The mental picture of uncertainty, generated in the older mind, perhaps through fear of some particular danger to which the child is supposed to have been subjected, is reflected in the delicate nervous system, and corresponding vibrations of discord register in the physical system—the child is taken sick in consequence. This effect is generally attributed to the weather, the food, or to the supposed presence in the atmosphere of some particular thing called a disease, while the real enemy remains unrecognized.

Minds are mirrors to thought-pictures, and reflect perfectly every outline. The minds of intelligent children are the most keenly sensitive mirrors of this kind, responding instantly to either right or wrong thought-action. Because of this fact these helpless little victims are at the mercy of surrounding mental disturbances, unless a counteracting mental influence of a right character is brought to bear in their favor.

The appalling child mortality in many civilized communities marks through our otherwise enlightened land the blighted pathway of erroneous convictions in regard to the Thought of Evil. If entertained, this thought will inevitably result in the fear of death—or an end to life. This line of action contains mental images of distress which these sensitive little ones cannot endure, and because of its distressing vibrations they pass over the border in thousands.

Several types of contagious disease originate entirely within this malignant field of false Mental Imagery. The sub-conscious action of similar thought is extremely intricate in detail, yet one erroneous principle underlies its every exercise; that is, the picturing in mind of conceptions contrary to the harmonies of real life. The excuse that such thoughts are *believed* to be true will not in the smallest degree change or vary the inevitable result.

Every thought is a thing in mind, and throws out a reflection which must be like the mental action from which it proceeds. When people learn to think and picture in mind that which they wish to possess rather than that which they fear, this law will be employed for real and permanent good. The Law is inexorable: act against it, and you will suffer its penalties; co-operate with it and you will share its goodness.

The direct action of mind in and through the nervous system is the secret of what seems to be physical life. When it ceases, life leaves the body, but does not necessarily leave the mind; for mind is a living entity of spiritual substance, having an enduring nature independent of matter or physical form.

Spiritual activity is the only real Life, while Spirit is the one active element of Divine Reality in the Universe.

When used in relation to man, Mind and Spirit are terms employed to designate conscious activity on different planes of existence and in different phases of life. Spirit is the intelligent Individual, active in the higher forms and on all possible planes of intelligence and consciousness; while Mind is the same Individual acting on the thought-plane only. Continuing this classification, the Personality is that Individual acting temporarily on the sense-plane,—in the illusion of physical sensation; and the body is a physical machine, constructed by mind, of material elements, for the purpose of analyzing sensations on this plane. Being a part of the earth, the body never leaves it, yet it depends entirely upon mind for form, structure, action, power and organization.

He whose knowledge of his own being is limited to the outward objective laws of the physical body, knows nothing certain even about that organism;

while he who has acquired true knowledge of the foundation principles of life, operating through the spiritual action of thought, has an understanding of facts with regard to the activities of both mind and body; for the body is controlled entirely by mind, which re-enacts the fundamental activities of intelligence; while these, in turn, are produced by active spirit, the substantial principle of conscious life.

When spiritual life-action ceases to register in the nerves of the body, it begins to disintegrate and soon returns to its component elements of carbon, iron, salt, lime, soda, sulphur, phosphorus, magnesium, potash, saltpetre, water, hydrogen, oxygen, nitrogen, and other earth elements of which it is constructed, and in varying proportions of which it is held together during physical life, by super-conscious mental action. Whether it shall be retained in its natural proportion of ingredients and in normal degrees of action, depends upon the character of the mental action which governs it, while this, in turn, depends upon the active thought generated by the individual.

These facts are concentrated in the Proverb of Solomon: "For as he thinketh in his heart so is he,"* both physically and mentally, in fact.

* Proverbs xxiii : 7.

Thought contrary to natural law produces disease. Thought in accordance with nature's laws results in health. This principle is absolute and universal.

Where no mental action exists, no disease can take root. This statement is indisputable, if the fact of sub-conscious and super-conscious as well as conscious mental action be taken into consideration, as must be the case before any definite information in regard to either mind or body can be acquired.

Pure thought reflects in pure action:

Pure act reacts in harmonious sensation.

CHAPTER IX.

CURATIVE INFLUENCES.

What is a Mental Cure?

In Metaphysical Philosophy man is understood to be:

First—Spirit, a living intelligence, capable of thought for a conscious purpose; a living entity of spiritual essence and substance—eternal, indestructible, and not subject to physical injury or outward control.

Second—Mind, which is Spirit in the thinking process of living activity.

Third—Body, an outward expression of Mind in the evidence of sensation, through a physical system composed chiefly of millions of ganglia and nerves, combined in so intricate a system that its detail is almost beyond human comprehension; so infinite in number that even the point of a needle placed in contact with the skin sometimes covers not only a nerve, but a system of nerves too fine to be examined by material agency.

Nothing physical can be constructed fine enough to operate advantageously upon these infinitesimally small organs, to say nothing of influencing the vital fluid which flows through them. In construction they are finer than the molecular form of any drug. Man's physical senses are too coarse to come in contact with them, and his means for mechanical action are too large to operate upon them; his clumsy attempts can only interfere with Nature's mental handiwork. Yet these delicate instruments are of the most vital importance in every act of physical life, and direct curative influence is impossible except through some mode of their activity, controlled by thought.

The Ganglionic nerves are the immediate instruments of mind, responding to every conscious thought, as do the strings of a harp to atmospheric vibrations. Thought is more subtle than even these tiny organs, and they obey its every impulse.

In the attempt to heal, the conventional physician approaches the case from a material standpoint, reaching the physical body through the stomach by means of chemical action; therefore, he can at best hope to reach directly only those troubles which are distinctly associated with digestion and assimilation of food, with conditions of the blood and of those special organs the action of which depends upon the stomach.

Chemical action in the human stomach is not a fixed quantity, but varies with every person and changes with every emotion of the mind. Because of this fact, the effect of medicine can never be foretold with exactness, and every dose becomes an experiment. Mind is the Chemist that operates in the Laboratory of digestion, and through the activity of thought on all planes of consciousness the digestive apparatus is under absolute control of Intelligence.

The Metaphysician approaches the individual from a standpoint opposite that of the medical schools, considering him a Spiritual Being rather than a Thing composed mainly of material elements. Dealing with mind, he reaches the physical system through the brain and the ganglionic nervous system, rather than through the stomach,—entering at the front door and meeting his Host in the drawing-room instead of in the kitchen. Comprehensive understanding is the basis of operation rather than chemical fermentation. Appeal is made to the intelligent Soul on the plane of understanding, instead of to the personality on the plane of sensation; correct living action is thereby established in mind and super-consciously re-enacted in the Brain cells.

This condition is immediately transmitted through nerve circulation to all parts of the body, changing wrong modes of action in each organ to those which are right, and correcting every distorted function. Direct material action upon a particular organ is not necessary to this result.

Mind is the masterly regulator of the entire physical mechanism, and must therefore preside over every possible chemical action in all digestive processes; and if the right mental condition be established a corresponding physical condition becomes a matter of course.

In dealing with classified diseases by any physical process of cure, the distinctly nervous and mental forms give the physician the most trouble. To abandon the attempt to heal, shifting the responsibility to the patient with the statement that nothing is the matter—it is only "Imagination," is to confess entire ignorance as regards this remarkable faculty, by which strong men are often held in bondage.

It is puerile to say of any patient that his sickness is only imaginary,—a fault of his own which he might correct if he would. No sane man would intentionally bring suffering upon himself and consciously continue its action, and no insane person would be capable of deliberately producing such a result. Clearly something is wrong; and he the trouble real or "imaginary" it is the physician's duty to ascertain its nature, and to discover an adequate remedial agency.

If, perchance, the patient only imagines a trouble which is not present, there should be found a cure for that distorted imagination. Such a cure will never be discovered without a full understanding of what Imagination really is, and in what line of activity it originates.

The Imagination being a mental faculty, or, at least, an instrument of the mind, in order to gain the necessary information the mental activities must be investigated. Study along this line has been somewhat neglected by the medical schools, principally, perhaps, because mind has been viewed as an adjunct of the body, more or less physical in its nature: a vague something or other, probably seated in the brain, perchance the brain itself; and the statement is frequently heard that mind is incapable of action except in accordance with its existing physical conditions, as an instrument of the body. This opinion leads to the conclusion that mind is of no importance in a therapeutic sense, save that it should be kept quiet until the physical body can be healed through drug medication, when, it is supposed, the body will restore its own mind to the normal condition.

Metaphysical philosophy shows this view of the construction and control of man's natural system to be not only erroneous, but exactly a reversal of the facts of life.

Adequate study of all forms of sickness proves the existence of a mental origin for each case; therefore all maladies are mental rather than physical in their nature, being simply different degrees of mental distress registered in the physical system.

Continued experiment demonstrates the fact that all forms of disease may be cured by changing the order of the mental action from which they originally emanated.

This is what Metaphysical Healing accomplishes. It occupies a field where medical knowledge is inadequate, where materia medica is silent, and where medical practice is powerless to aid directly the millions who turn to it with confidence, in the hopeful expectation of scientific relief.

The subject of the mental nature and cure of disease is worthy of the most careful examination by every intelligent thinker. The history of medical practice shows that in the treatment of disease the experience of the competent physician leads him away from the administration of drugs. The most successful physicians of the present day employ the least number and the smallest quantity of medicines—frequently none, even in severe cases. Why? "The less there is employed of the *right remedy* the better the result produced!" Such is the logic derived from these facts of practice.

In the hope of finding possible remedies, experiment has been made with almost every known element of the earth; and every minute part of the physical system has been examined, in order to discover its material rules of action. Yet to-day materia medica has no remedy for any sympathetic nervous disease, except some drug which intensifies nervous action often to the point of destroying the finer parts of the nervous system, or stupefies the faculties by partially paralyzing what yet remains undestroyed of that intricate system of finest nerves which are of most vital importance in physical existence: in fact, all the more important because too fine in construction to be examined through the instruments of sensation.

This line of experiment frequently terminates in what perhaps is attributed to the supposed fatality of an existing disease. The result was really brought about, however, through the presence of a foreign element introduced into the system, an element which destroyed the natural action that it was expected to restore, while the real cause passed unrecognized. Of course, the harm is unintentional, and the disastrous result deplored, perhaps in an agony of regrets, by the physician as well as by the patient's friends, but the error is none the less fatal for that reason.

Under the theory of drug medication, when an organ or a function is unnaturally excited, the physician aims to depress the nervous system and to discourage action, thereby to reduce vitality, until disturbance shall cease. When action is subnormal, the aim is to intensify action by means of a stimulant or other excitant, which causes an equally unnatural mode of molecular motion in the disturbed parts without in any degree increasing the amount of vitality present in the system.

In either of these attempts to heal, the final result is a reduction of the vitality registered in the physical system; because all poisons injure, and most drugs destroy, some part of the finer nervous mechanism, thereby rendering the instrument imperfect, so that Mind, the real and intelligent operator—the only source of vitality in the human body—cannot register its highest and best modes of activity. As with a harp or piano, when the strings belonging to any notes are broken, those tones can no longer be produced, be the operator ever so skillful.

The nervous system is the physical mechanism through which mind outwardly expresses its thoughts and registers its modes of action in the body. No person can physically live a moment without a nervous system. No one can be actively intelligent on this life plane without the most finely constructed nervous system, in perfect condition and fully operative. Every nerve dispensed with means a corresponding degree of physical power sacrificed, and under some circumstances lost, during the remainder of this life-period.

For every material element contained in the earth there is a corresponding mental element, or a mode of activity in Universal Mind; the correspondence is exact and the laws run parallel.

Every drug is accompanied by a mode of subconscious mental activity of a degraded order, which is so foreign to the nature of the mental organism and to the natural construction and operation of the higher divisions of the nervous mechanism, that normal action is impossible while it is present. The physical and the mental of a parallel grade accompany each other: moral and physical degradation go hand in hand. The inevitable moral degradation of those addicted to the habitual use of either alcohol or opium illustrates this principle.

The average patient expects that the drug administered will act with curative effect upon the disease which is supposed to be present, and believes that alcohol and other drugs possess substance and sustaining power which are needed in reconstructing the depleted system. But, in fact, healthy tissue is built only by nature and from natural food ingredients,—never in any instance from a poisonous preparation. Every drug is a poison, which enters the circulation in the same manner as other poisons. Nature rejects unnatural ingredients and expels them from every part of the physical system by the most energetic means, because they are useless in the construction of healthy tissue. They are *against*, not *for*, health. The atomic construction and molecular form of drugs is unlike that of any part of the human system. There is no health either in a poison or in any of its attendant effects.

The tremendous effort made by nature to eject from the system any foreign element of a poisonous character sometimes leads to the erroneous conclusion that the element contains in itself genuine power-producing forces, which are adapted to establish natural action and to restore health. On the contrary, the system is frequently depleted of its vitality by the serious drain made upon it in disposing of the useless element, resulting in harm which more than counterbalances any good that could be expected from distorted action inevitably following the introduction of a drug.

If for any reason nature fails to eject the drug introduced, mind deserts the physical system, because it has been rendered unfit for its purpose.

Drugs frequently change molecular construction in either blood or nerve fluid by destroying the molecules themselves, thereby producing chemical combinations for which nature has no use, and depriving the system of its natural sustenance. In this condition mental action, whether right or wrong, can not clearly express itself, and so temporary relief in mere sensation is sometimes gained, though at the cost of partial destruction of the most important nerves.

If the fact was generally understood that in the physical body any degree of action necessary to the restoration of health may readily be produced through rightly directed thought energy, this worse-than-useless forcing of the vital organs into distressing modes of action would cease, and many valuable lives would be prolonged for future usefulness.

People remain under the unhappy influences of disease and drugs only because the true laws of life are unknown to them. False opinions with regard to the nature, scope and power of disease and its true remedies almost universally prevail, because erroneous ideas of life based upon a *physical structure only* are commonly taught. These ideas have developed almost imperceptibly during study of the *controlled* body as the real man, instead of the *controlling* mind. This study has been pursued entirely upon the inadequate and unreliable evidence of the five physical senses, while the permanent activities of the individual and his more reliable senses of higher perception have been largely ignored. Information thus gained is incomplete and, if trusted literally, will be misleading in many ways.

The fallacious theory that healthy tissue can be produced either from or because of the presence of that which can only result in destruction of tissue, has already filled uncounted millions of untimely graves. Will you, intelligent reader, allow this theory to mislead you, or will you don the cap of logic and the coat of reasonable analysis, enter the field of investigation, and learn for yourself the principles because of which you live, and the laws of mental action through which your physical system has been developed? If you learn these truths thoroughly, disease will lose the terrors of its supposed power over you and yours, and untimely death will cease to haunt you as a possible outcome of nearly every simple act of life.

Effort to cure nervous troubles will generally result in failure until adequate study of the Mental mechanism and its Spiritual faculties is accomplished, when it will be discovered that the body is an adjunct of the mind, not *vice versa* as frequently supposed, and that it is built and sustained by mind, which is the controlling element under all circumstances. In fact it has already been proved in thousands of careful experiments that Mind is a living, intelligent Entity, having a nature, a system and a life of its own. The body reflects mental activity in physical element, and thus is built, partly destroyed or reconstructed, according as mind changes its modes of action.

Mind is the Intelligence of the body. Mind thinks: its Thought is registered on the body in physical element. The thought is a model of the idea; the body and its conditions are a constructed copy of the model. When the model changes, the copy correspondingly changes. This rule holds good with regard to every part of the system, but is especially true of the most finely constructed parts, because these are subject to the quickest changes. In the finest nerve mechanism important changes frequently occur instantaneously, while in the coarser structure of bone, cartilage and ligament, they take place more slowly.

The instant the mental cause ceases its disturbing vibrations nature begins natural restorative activity in every part of the physical system; this is as certain as that water will run down hill. All that is necessary, then, is that a correct diagnosis of the Mental Influences be obtained and that the mental changes be rightly produced by an understanding mind.

In this perfectly natural way any case of sickness is curable by metaphysical treatment, provided there still remains enough of the substructure for nature to build upon. Unless there be something for nature to work upon, cure of that case by any means is manifestly impossible.

When these truths are intelligently comprehended the fact becomes evident that disease—whatever its name or nature — must originate in some mental activity afterwards registered in the body, where that mode of action is outwardly expressed. Knowledge of this fact is the key to accurate diagnostication and a sure guide to an adequate Mental Therapeutics. In such understanding, mind possesses most valuable powers, alike prophylactic, pathological, and therapeutical.

The discovery of this eternal fact in regard to man's mental and physical structure is an electric search-light thrown upon this hitherto darkened field of inquiry. By understanding clearly how mind acts to produce conditions of disease, and how it may be led to act in an opposite direction to result in health, the right remedies for all the ills to which flesh has been supposed to be heir become evident.

Through knowledge of the natural laws of human existence, based upon intelligent understanding of the fundamental principles of Spiritual Life, each thinking mind has power to reverse every wrong mode of action and to establish right conditions. Exercise of this power in removing disease is a legitimate Mental Cure. Its nature is Metaphysical.

CHAPTER X.

THE PHYSICAL EFFECTS OF ANGER.

How Mental Action Causes Disease.

THE mental state commonly known as anger forcibly illustrates the line of action in which mind produces physical results.

The English word Anger is derived from the Latin *angor*, which means "Compression of the neck; strangling; from *angere*, to press together; to choke, especially of the mind; to torture; to vex."

Anger is a passionate emotion of the mind. It is expressed in various degrees of intensity, ranging from slight fear of loss or other harm because of supposed injustice, to the most furious degree of rage, based upon imaginary hatred of another.

Hatred is a false element which possesses no genuine *quality* and is destitute of *principle*. Rage, when forced to its final limits, ends in impotence; this proves its native nothingness.

Anger has no harmonious modes of action. It originates on the lower plane of sense-existence, and is brutal in its nature. Definite physical conditions invariably follow the mental act. To test this statement, analyze both the mental and physical conditions of an angry person and note the correspondence existing between the two.

In cases of extreme anger, the eyes violently snap in discord, the jaws are set and the teeth grind together expressing the thought of destruction indulged in mind. The hands clench and the fingers clutch convulsively, evincing an inclination to destroy the object of supposed hatred. All muscles are tense, strained and abnormal, while their action is acute in nature, angular in character, destructive in intention and tendency. Every faculty and every function is distorted.

Under the influence of anger the action of the heart is also seriously disturbed. It beats in convulsive throbbings, forcing destructive modes of motion upon the blood corpuscles, which modes in turn are conveyed to every vital organ. The face either flushes or pales, as blood is forced to the surface or withdrawn to the internal organs in congestion. Digestive processes are instantly checked, and do not proceed until natural circulation of the blood is restored. The kidneys secrete acids generated by the destruction of natural blood corpuscles; these acids bear direct correspondence to the false and destructive character of vengeful thoughts.

The lungs contract unnaturally and move in spasmodic gasps, in which every breathing function is either paralyzed or distorted, resulting in serious interference with respiration. In healthy action the lungs perform the final process of digestion by oxygenation of the digested food before it passes into the blood for use in building new tissue. During healthy activity, which proceeds naturally from harmonious thought, an abundance of pure oxygen is extracted from the air inhaled and perfect digestion ensues; but, during the inverted action which results from indulgence of angry thought, oxygen is discarded, while Nitrogen is generated and retained beyond its normal proportion; thus interfering with the most important part of the process of digestion and assimilation, to the future detriment of every organ and function of the physical system. If a state of angry feeling or ill temper be allowed to become chronic, a similar disturbance of some or all of the vital, digestive, secretive and excretive organs and functions ensues. Disease of all kinds is generated spontaneously under these inharmonious conditions.

While responding to angry influence every muscle of the body is under tension, and drawn to some extent out of its natural position. If anger be continued, muscular tension persists, followed by chronic contraction, with or without painful sensation, according to circumstances. Muscular rheumatism is frequently generated in this manner. Any line of mental action which places the muscles under continuous tension may result in some form of muscular rheumatism. Fright frequently becomes an active cause of acute rheumatism, which will assume muscular forms if the reflected mental action places the muscles under tension; or inflammatory forms if the picture carries in its activity the element of burning, as in a mental picture of flames or any intensely inflammatory thought. The details of the symptoms vary with the different causes, but the principles involved are identical.

Under the influence of anger, the spasmodic muscular distortions of the heart produce violent valvular agitation, which is the exact representation of some forms of action in cases of valvular disease of the heart. If the disturbing cause be perpetuated, the valves continue to register the wrong action until it finally becomes a fixed habit, and some form of valvular disease becomes established. The first physical stage of this disease is functional, but if not arrested it finally develops to organic.

All forms of heart disease, including rheumatism of the heart, are caused by certain modes of mental action, generated by anger, fear, or some other abnormal emotion. The final symptoms are the direct result of the particular form of action established and continued, let the cause of that action be what it may. · In the final analysis of Anger we always find Fear as its foundation. These two emotions are closely allied.

The direct action of the heart upon the blood is a point worthy of serious consideration here, because disturbance of the circulation affects all vital organs and interferes with every physical function. Anger, reflected in explosive heart throbs, resembling blows given under impulse of hatred, fires the blood with poison passion, which explodes molecules, destroys blood corpuscles, and decomposes tissue, generating chemical combinations unnatural and injurious to the entire physical structure. If abnormal action of the heart continues a fever may develop, with characteristics corresponding to the nature of the causative mental action, whether it be anger, fear, excitement, worry or grief. All these mental states result in fever under suitable conditions. An abnormal degree of temperature and rate of the pulse are direct physical effects of distorted mental emotion.

Destructive modes of action established in the blood immediately extend to those vital organs which, in their action, respond to the mental faculties that were involved in the wrong thought, and a corresponding disturbance is likely to develop within that organ.

Interference with the natural action of the liver causes the secretion of a poisonous bile which, in character, corresponds exactly to the angry nature of the original cause of the disturbance. Because of direct reaction upon the liver through the blood, malarial symptoms are a common outcome of anger, fear, grief, dread, or protracted worry.

Bilious, typhoid and puerperal fevers frequently follow directly upon some violent outbreak of temper, either on the part of the patient or of some associate. Fright or great fear, particularly if accompanied by rage, may produce the same result. Fright prepares the way by undermining the nervous forces and weakening resistance, when an experience of anger may precipitate the trouble and determine the particular features of the disease to become established. In this event Fright would be the *predisposing* cause, and Anger the *precipitating* cause of the bilious or malarial attack.

Unless counteracted by a change of mental action, acids generated in the blood through chemical decomposition eventually destroy the natural secretive powers of the kidneys, which results in muscular degeneration, and develops kidney diseases as the ultimate of destructive action. Extreme fright and protracted worry also frequently produce this result.

The physical action established while yielding to angry impulse is a natural outcome of the thought indulged, while the corresponding disease is the immediate result of the particular thought-action. The mental condition is registered and re-enacted in the nervous system, producing its perfect copy in this as in other phases of human existence. The Body does not make the mind angry, but the Mind causes the body to re-enact the morbid state generated by wrong thought.

It is imperative that distorted thought should pass away before the body can cease to register and express distorted action. Attempt to remedy the bodily conditions first is not only a waste of effort, but, if persisted in, may result disastrously.

The disease caused by anger is a physical condition resulting from a previously established mental state. What is the right remedy? In a cure of the bodily condition the muscles must relax, the jaws loosen, the eyes become quiet, and again express kindly thoughts; natural color should return to the face, and the agitated, trembling, nervous system once more become tranquil. How shall we proceed to bring about these results? Shall we rub the tense muscles with oil or with liniment to loosen them, pry open the set jaws and lubricate their joints, or sever a muscle in the eye to stop its angry snap? Shall we put some drug in the stomach to complete the destruction of blood corpuscles, when the disturbance is already as great as the system can bear, or paralyze the heart to arrest its spasmodic movements?

"Ridiculous!" is probably the exclamation of many who read these questions; yet corresponding acts are performed every day in cases of illness where the mental cause is equally evident, and would be readily recognized if the actual state of mind was duly considered. The proper cure for every case of this kind in any stage of its development lies not in treating physical results but in re-establishing correct mental action.

How, then, may a mental remedy be applied? In the *simplest form* some quiet words should be spoken in a pleasant manner, and in a tone of voice as nearly opposite in character to the morbid state of mind as possible. Frequently under such influence the mental state soon changes, the anger begins to fade, the eye quiets, the muscles relax, the set jaws resume their natural position, the heart ceases to throb and gradually resumes its normal action, the rate of the pulse is reduced, color returns to the surface of the skin, and natural action eventually results in every part of the body. Why? Because Anger has ceased in mind, and there is no longer any element present to control the body through discord. The natural force of Love and attraction is allowed to resume its harmonious sway. The physical organs *are obliged* to respond to the natural action now re-established in mind—they have no choice in the matter.

If, however, after due persuasion, quiet words are not heeded and angry thought still continues, then Metaphysical Influence may be directly applied, accomplishing what nothing else can. Silently that disturbed mind may be reached by *thoughts of calm*, which, through the natural laws of mutual attraction, will compel it to listen and to cease its useless controversy.

In metaphysical treatment the mind is reached on the spiritual plane of Intelligence, where the attraction of love for all humanity prevails, in perfect sympathy with every troubled soul, and where anger is forever unknown. The angry person was acting on the sensation plane, that of self-will, where thought is temporarily brutalized in selfish act. Because of the repellent nature of this kind of thought, he impulsively resists every effort to approach him consciously, with an idea different from his present indulgence, if it be expressed in spoken words; but when Intelligence is appealed to in silent thought above the brute-will plane, his higher nature responds; he ceases angry thought, and the good result is already accomplished.

The opinion is commonly expressed that the result of anger is only a temporary condition of discord in body—not a settled physical disease. The reply is: Anger is a mental condition of *dis-ease*,—the literal root-meaning of the word disease,—and if allowed to continue, it settles into a chronic mental state, capable of developing to any degree of intensity. Through the natural correspondence of physical condition with mental activity, a definite form of disease is thereby established in the body. This disease is mental in nature as well as in origin; therefore the most natural cure would seem to be the removal from mind of the thought of hatred, anger, fear, terror, or any mental discord which generated the wrong physical action from which the disease emanated. Experience proves that when this is accomplished the disease immediately begins to decrease, as when steam is shut off from an engine the machinery instantly begins to reduce speed and will eventually stop for want of motive power.

Fear is a painful mental emotion.

Anger is a passionate mental discord.

Disease is a conscious morbid distress.

Mind is a necessary factor in emotion, passion or consciousness; therefore, fear, anger and disease can not originate apart from mind or without mental action.

Disease may originate without conscious recognition of its accompanying mental action; but if mind be *entirely absent* it does not even begin to develop. If there is no thought, there can be no disease.

Mind is matter's motive power; Thought, its active impulse.

CHAPTER XI.

THE INFLUENCE OF FEAR IN SICKNESS.

Discordant Emotion and Its Results.

Most persons know instinctively that it is best not to be afraid, but comparatively few are aware that Fear actually results in physical disease. Yet this fact has been repeatedly proved in Metaphysical practice by cases where the removal of the mental image producing some overpowering degree of fear was followed by permanent relief from a physical ailment which had been pronounced incurable.

This subject is worthy of patient examination by all thinkers. It is of vital importance, though commonly set aside with the remark: "Yes, I know that fear sometimes makes sick people worse, because they are already nervous and imaginative, and it is always well not to be afraid. But I am not imaginative nor hysterical; *my* sickness is a real physical disease, and fear has nothing to do with it. I am not afraid of anything, yet I am sick; consequently, the theory does not apply to *my* case or to any real sickness; it can apply only to persons of weak minds and doubtful intelligence, who simply imagine themselves sick."

These and similar remarks are heard constantly by all mental healers. They are honestly made, and to the speakers seem conclusive; but the opinions thus expressed indicate that the term *Fear* as used with reference to sickness, as well as the character and scope of its action, together with the nature and origin of disease, are entirely misunderstood.

Haste in drawing conclusions on this subject is the greatest mistake that can be made. The subject contains truths of great and universal importance, while the principles involved lie at every door and bear directly upon each life in almost every detail of experience; and this because *Fear* in some degree abounds everywhere, and every life is in some measure influenced by its destructive action. The only safety lies in knowing the nature and cause of its action, and in understanding how to avoid or how to counteract its baneful influence.

Every sick person is either consciously or subconsciously under the influence of the mental image of some experience, which at the time of its occurrence generated discordant mental emotion of some kind—perhaps fear in some degree, either in his own mind or in that of some person from whom it was received through the reflection of the mental image. This is not always conscious fear. There are numerous activities in mind of which we are not immediately conscious, and many forms of fear that are not recognized as such—in fact, are not recognized at all save through the outward effect in corresponding physical agitation.

Fear is a mental emotion, based upon lack of confidence or apprehension of injury or danger. It has many degrees, varying all the way from slight dissatisfaction down through grades of discontent and unhappiness, doubt, apprehension, solicitude, anxiety, worry, dread, repulsion, loathing, hatred, anger, horror, hopelessness, fright, terror, shock—perhaps followed by insensibility or total unconsciousness on the physical plane, the ultimate of which is the state spoken of as death.

All these emotions are direct results of the varying degrees of fear. Each shares the general characteristics of the state known as *being afraid of* something; for the objective point of each similar state of mind is some thing, person, influence or action not desired, and hence feared in direct ratio to its undesirability. The existing mental state is frequently the result of thought applied to that subject with relation to its probable effect on the happiness of one's own life, or perhaps indirectly, on the happiness of another. It is an emotional state of mental unrest, unease, disquiet—that is, of dis-ease.

A thought of disquiet will register as physical un-ease, and corresponding sensations will pulsate through the finest nerves. If severe or long-continued, this condition of unrest or disquietude settles into nervous dis-ease and a Disease of the nerves becomes established. This disturbed condition of the circulation of nerve fluids is transferred to and correspondingly registered in the blood circulation, and diseases of the blood ensue. These register on the vital organs and through the various tissues of the body, producing with different physical systems every variety of disease. The detail of each disease varies according to individual circumstances, but all bear direct relation to the corresponding degree of the mental emotion of fear by which they were generated.

Some physicians deny these facts; but those who have had large experience recognize that, in some inexplicable manner, fear does sometimes cause sickness. They usually argue, however, that when it has become established, the organic disease is an independent physical thing, and a material remedy must be administered in order to produce a cure. This conclusion is inconsistent with the premise, and illogical in view of demonstrated facts. Similar opinions prevail, because the universal laws through which mind controls the nervous system are not well understood. The fertile field of Mental Therapeutics has not been investigated to any appreciable extent by these thinkers; therefore, a material remedy for the apparently physical disease is considered a necessity.

Mind acting on the super-conscious plane of natural activity builds its own body in healthy tissue and keeps it strong. But in acting sub-consciously through fear each mind partially unbuilds its body by modes of action which correspond to the uncertain thought entertained.

If mind, through fear, loses self-control and becomes completely absorbed in the thought of destruction, it literally deserts its body because of the fright occasioned by the mental picture of death by accident. This was entirely unnecessary, and if the thought-picture had not been formed it would not have occurred. If this picture had been changed or removed, there would have remained no incentive to the act.

If the body is rendered a useless machine by injury, Mind, its active intelligence, deserts it; this is commonly called death. The physician frequently attributes this change to heart disease or "heart failure." The question, for an answer to which the people look to Science, is, Why did that heart fail at that particular time? Until the advocates of Materia Medica can answer this question intelligently, with a real remedy for unnecessary occurrences of the kind, their therapeutics has no claim to be considered an exact science, and no moral right to exclusive practice. Metaphysics answers this question, with an application of principles which releases many a victim from hitherto unrecognized influences which have been hastening him over the border, while medical science confidently signed the death warrant.

Through knowledge, mind has control of its body, and may carry it safely through many of the occurrences which would otherwise result in bringing life on the physical plane to an untimely end.

In the practice of Metaphysical Healing this theory has been successfully applied in thousands of instances, all the evidence of which goes to prove that if the fear or mental unrest which originated the physical condition be removed the mental action soon changes, its reflection in the nervous system disappears, and, as a natural consequence, nerve circulation is re-established. The Brain becomes quiet, the rate of the pulse returns to the normal, the temperature is oftentimes reduced almost immediately, respiration becomes natural, sleep returns under the quieting influence of pure and restful Thought, digestion is improved and finally restored, whereupon perfect assimilation is followed by natural rebuilding of every part of the system.

Super-conscious mental action is the only reconstructive agency. Nature, which is Universal Mind in harmonious action on the super-conscious plane, is always ready to begin natural restorative processes the instant that obstructions to her modes of action are removed.

Knowledge of Metaphysical Principles enables one to begin immediately the removal of mental obstructions, and aids in establishing mental quiet, cheerfulness, courage and hope. With these conditions present, Nature again assumes her sway and life renews the vigor of the system.

When once entered upon, Metaphysical diagnostication for mental causes of nervous and physical diseases becomes an extremely interesting study. The investigation is most fascinating, not only because an insight is gained into the nature of these disturbances, but also because the intricate workings of the mental mechanism are so clearly defined through the Imaging process of Thought as to compel astonishment at the extent, rapidity, intensity and endurance of Thought-activity, as well as at the infinite variety of results produced by its reflection.

The immediate correspondence between the Thought-picture and its physical copy in the nervous system is an exceedingly interesting and important feature of diagnostication.

The line of Thought-activity which caused the sickness will be in some measure like the sickness itself; *i.e.*, in some one or more ways the same modes of action will exist in both the mental cause and the physical effect—the same laws of activity will be manifested in each. This resemblance one to the other is always marked, and often exact in every particular. Frequently the mental action is very intense; then the physical agitation is severe and the accompanying sensations correspondingly acute in their appearance. Each mode of action appearing in any physical condition accurately denotes a Law involved in the mental act from which that condition proceeds. The degree of intensity is always modified somewhat, though never wholly changed, by the mental nature of the individual.

Every distinct feature of the bodily ailment is an

exact copy of the Mental Image of some one or more features in a Thought-picture existing in the mind of the sufferer, either from direct thought, conscious or sub-conscious, or reflected there from thought-activity generated in other minds. If this picture had not been formed in mind, or its reflection had not been absorbed, the sickness could not have occurred; if its action can be made to cease the sickness will disappear. With an adequate understanding of the principles involved in these facts it becomes possible to trace back directly from the physical symptom to the corresponding mental emotion which caused it. This once removed, the road to recovery is easy and certain.

The natural steps in this Thought-process are as follows:

(*a*) In conscious thought a Mental Picture is developed.

(*b*) The mental picture is reflected, producing Nervous Action.

(*c*) That Action is registered in and through the tissue of the physical body.

(*d*) A corresponding bodily condition, more or less permanent, is the inevitable result.

Many people have experienced fear, the remembrance of which causes a chill to pass along the spine, a cold perspiration to start, or a shudder to vibrate through the system. Some people faint repeatedly for no other reason than the sub-conscious recurrence in mind of a past fearful experience; others feel dizzy, and inclined to fall, for the same reason. It is common to hear such expressions as "It makes me shudder to think of the danger," "I tremble at the remembrance of that situation," "My heart sinks at the thought of how near death came to me," "My teeth chatter at the very sound," "I dream of a similar occurrence and awake in fright," and others of like character.

In many such cases the season of the year, the day of the month or week, or the particular hour of day or night at which an accident happened, act as a coincidence to call the picture into sub-conscious action. Thereupon the original fear returns and an attack of illness is experienced which is the immediate result of that disturbed nervous action, and bears direct correspondence to the particular picture formed at the moment of the accident. Nearly every acute disease is generated in this manner through laws of corresponding mental action.

All the earnest physicians of the civilized world are searching through every substance upon earth, in all possible combinations, for material remedies for these diseases. Think you such will be found? Not while the imaging faculty of mind continues to register and retain the features of scenes of fright. So long as Mental Imaging continues to be the law of mental action the nervous system will persist in expressing a nervous copy of the mental impression, and the best of humanity—because the most sensitive and responsive —will continue to slip through the fingers of Materia Medica practitioners in spite of experience, skill and watchful care, together with consultations of learned men and concoction of remedies without number.

This is not in any particular an overdrawn picture or an exaggerated statement. It is the common experience of all civilized communities. Millions annually pass from this plane of life for no other reason than that the imaging faculty of the human mind and its natural effects are not understood, while other millions live but to suffer the torture of harassing thought-pictures generated either in physical accidents or in morally wrong lines of thought-action.

A striking illustration of the effect of an impression left upon the mind by a scene of terror is contained in an experience of the late Charles Dickens, an account of which is given in the concluding installment of an extremely interesting reminiscent series of six papers, entitled "My Father As I Recall Him," by Mamie Dickens.*

In the number for April, 1893, Miss Dickens writes: "It was while on his way home . . . that he was in the railroad accident to which he alludes in a letter which I quoted in the last number of these reminiscences, saying that his heart had never been in good condition since that accident. It occurred on the ninth of June, a date which, five years later, was the day of his death." Then follows a letter written by himself, describing in detail the accident from which he escaped in a marvelous way: "I have —I don't know what to call it—constitutional (I suppose) presence of mind, and was not in the least fluttered at the time, but in writing these scanty words of recollection I feel the shake and am obliged to stop." Miss Dickens further explains: "We heard afterwards how helpful he had been at the time, ministering to the dying! How calmly and tenderly he cared for the suffering ones about him! But he never entirely recovered from the shock." More than a year later the novelist wrote:

"It is remarkable that my watch (a special chronometer) has never gone quite correctly since, and to this day there sometimes comes over me, on a

---

* Published in "The Ladies' Home Journal," Philadelphia, Pa.

railway train or any sort of conveyance, for a few seconds, a vague sense of dread that I have no power to check. It comes and passes, but I can not prevent its coming."

Miss Dickens adds: "I have often seen this dread come upon him; and on one occasion . . . my father suddenly clutched the arms of the railway-carriage seat while his face grew ashy pale and great drops of perspiration stood upon his forehead; and though he tried to master the dread, it was so strong that he had to leave the train at the next station. The accident had left its impression upon the memory, and it was destined never to be effaced. The hours spent upon railroads were thereafter often hours of pain to him. I realized this often while traveling with him, and no amount of assurance could dispel the feeling."

In this account it is clearly evident that this accident was considered the cause of his nervous trepidation and of the suffering which no one could then relieve.

To quote again from the same paper, in regard to his last hours: "He made an earnest effort to struggle against the seizure which was fast coming over him, and continued to talk, but incoherently and very indistinctly. It being now evident that he was in a serious condition, my aunt begged him to go to his room . . . 'Come and lie down,' she entreated. 'Yes, *on the ground,*' he answered, indistinctly. These were the last words that he uttered as he sank to the floor. On the following day . . . with a shudder, a deep sigh, and a large tear rolling down his cheek, his spirit left us—the evening of the ninth."

To those who understand the natural effect of mental pictures of distress, every feature of the last scene in Mr. Dickens's life corresponds clearly to the mental experience of that accidental occurrence.

The entire scene was retained in his mind as a picture. As the anniversary approached this picture became intensely active—perhaps he had been consciously thinking over the scene. Reaching the absolute degree of realization, it was reflected in his nervous system in imitation of the scene. The first feature of the picture was the fright which occurred at the moment of the accident. This was clearly expressed in his sudden attack of illness. The next feature was the mental shock from horror at the devastation and destruction of human life, with the picture of people dying while *lying upon the ground*, and whom he was helpless to save. This was clearly expressed in his last words, given in response to the request to lie down, "Yes, on the ground," although he was then in the house. At the last moment the self-centering of the ultimate realization of death scenes in the accident is so clearly expressed in the shudder of horror, the sigh of hopelessness, and the large tear of sympathy, that there is little doubt but that his soul passed from this life during and because of subconscious realization to the ultimate degree of the scene of the accident from which he could not escape.

Mental Imagery of the incidents and experiences of life, with its inevitable effects on the entire physical system, regardless of conscious recognition by the individual, has now become a well-attested fact, and it is also certain that, by acting in accordance with the laws of Mental Healing, all injurious mental impressions can be permanently effaced, and their after-effects avoided.

This is the scientific ground upon which Metaphysical Healing stands, and the field of action in which to-day a nobler work is being performed for the human race than has ever before been exhibited to the world. Its beneficial power is not limited to the healing of bodily ailments, neither will its action cease when the last cure is effected. The principles of life involved in metaphysical healing extend to every moral action, and cover the entire diapason of active life in the Mind, Soul and Spirit of the human individual. Its importance, therefore, can not be overestimated.

THE REMEDY FOR EVERY INHARMONIOUS STATE IS FOUND IN A REVERSAL OF THE ACTION WHICH PRODUCED IT.

Incorrect Thought develops wrong Action, which must inevitably come to an end. Correct Thought establishes right Activity, which will endure forever in harmonious life on the spiritual plane.

Reality is Eternal.

CHAPTER XII.

ILLUSTRATIVE CASES.

Cures that Have Been Effected.

A FEW cases have been selected from among hundreds that have occurred in practice to illustrate the kind of thought-action in which disease generates. All depend upon the same fundamental laws of mental activity, varying only in individual circumstances. The evidence accumulated by experience with such cases proves beyond question that mind images every conscious Idea, and that those Ideas which relate to self-existence are re-enacted in the physical system.

CASE OF A.—This man, about thirty-five years of age, suffered from a dull pain in one leg above the ankle, described as feeling like a broken bone. At times the spot was inflamed and swollen, with increased pain. A marked feature of the case was that on starting suddenly to catch a street car or a train, the sensation would instantly change from dull to acute pain, with such intensity as frequently to compel a stop.

Inquiry revealed the following facts: About twelve years previous to this examination, he was standing on the platform of a railroad station while a passenger train was pulling out. When the train was well under way, a man came hastily from the waiting-room and attempted to get on board. He fell, and a wheel took one leg off above the ankle. A was the first to reach the sufferer and render assistance. There were especially distressing features connected with the scene; but it was subsequently forgotten, and had not been consciously recalled for several years. Although not consciously remembered, this scene remained active sub-consciously, and caused the suffering previously described.

Physical treatment had no remedial effect. Yet when the sudden fright caused by seeing another in danger was erased from his mind immediate relief followed; and within a few weeks every sign of the trouble disappeared. Nine years have elapsed, with no return of the symptoms.

This case fairly illustrates the kind of mental action which causes disease. At the time of the accident the observer, while too far away to render precautionary assistance, was yet within ready view of every movement. Recognizing the danger, every mental emotion was at once called into intense activity, and a mental photograph embodying every detail of the scene was instantaneously impressed upon mind, exactly as in the act of material photography. This Picture remained clearly delineated in the substance of Mind, being always present though not continuously recognized, in the same manner as the picture remains on the photographer's plate, though it be for months out of sight and remembrance. So complete a coincidence as running for a car instantaneously called the entire picture into intense activity; and acute pain, reflecting from the keen sense of danger sub-consciously imagined as present, at once throbbed through the nerves of the part which was the subject of injury in the original picture. At times sufficient agitation of tissue developed to result in inflammation. Conscious memory is not a necessary factor in this line of mental action.

Through a process of conscious thought, based upon correct understanding of the laws of existence, metaphysical treatment causes such needless action to cease. When this is accomplished fear vanishes, and the sub-conscious illusion of continually living in a previous scene, with the accompanying false idea of danger, disappears. Thereupon its reflection in the physical tissue fades, and nature restores the usual health. This is a Metaphysical Cure. It is strictly scientific in character, because, with exact knowledge in regard to both cause and effect, it strikes directly at the root of the trouble and cures at once, knowing what is to be done, how it is done, and why it should be done. Other methods are attempts to cure by influencing the imagination through some form of emotion, through faith in some outside power to do the work, or through a blind belief in the efficacy of a drug, which arouses some degree of imagination in the direction of a cure, while nature does the work.

While some recover under all methods of treatment, owing partly to nature's tremendous recuperative powers, others succumb to the constantly active and unperceived influence of the original Mental Picture of distress. Still others pass away because unable to withstand the injurious influence of a foreign element introduced into the physical system as a remedy for a mental condition which is forever beyond the reach of anything more material than Thought itself.

CASE OF B.—This was a young woman whose case had been medically diagnosticated as Bronchial Consumption. It did not yield to medical treatment. The patient was weak and nervous, with little endurance, a severe cough, bronchial and catarrhal inflammation with throat complications, and extreme sensitiveness to moisture in the atmosphere. When questioned, she explained that she coughed because of a feeling as though there was sand in the windpipe. She was attacked by frequent severe bronchial colds. The patient, her friends and her physician were completely discouraged.

It was learned that a few weeks before the first cold which led up to the described condition, she was drowned to the extent of unconsciousness while surf-bathing. There were mental complications requiring continued treatment for a while, but this drowning was the original and the principal cause. The subconscious idea that she was continually re-enacting that scene of danger was removed through metaphysical treatment. Speedy relief followed, and in a few weeks the symptoms disappeared; within three months her usual health was fully restored. Seven years have elapsed since the treatment, giving sufficient time to test the permanence of the cure.

This woman, naturally strong and ambitious, was rapidly passing beyond the line of physical endurance because of the influence of a mental picture of expected death from a past experience, in which no physical danger any longer existed. The trouble was not the continuation of a physical injury, but continuance of the mental impression of death which was formed during the accident, with its definite picture of water and sand as the means of destruction. In other words, it was not death, but the Thought of death,—a false Idea which was constantly at work underneath, reproducing itself in the physical tissue, undermining health, and rapidly leading to the ultimate of its disturbing action.

Drowning scenes produce every variety of disease of the respiratory organs, because the idea of danger is centered there, through fear of injury by inhaling a destructive foreign element. This thought continuing in sub-conscious action becomes the cause of repeated attacks of nervous agitation. The only adequate curative influence is such as will remove the mental impression of danger and its consequent fear. To exercise such an influence is declared by many who are considered the world's greatest thinkers to be beyond human capability. Nevertheless, its exercise is an established fact of daily occurrence, and may be performed with some degree of success by any rightly informed individual.

The necessity for some means of assistance for the mentally afflicted is suggested in the dialogue between Macbeth and his wife's physician:

Macb. "How does your patient, doctor?"

Doct. "Not so sick, my lord,
As she is troubled with thick-coming fancies,
That keep her from her rest."

Macb. "Cure her of that.
Canst thou not minister to a mind diseas'd?
Pluck from the memory a rooted sorrow,
Raze out the written troubles of the brain,
And with some sweet, oblivious antidote
Cleanse the stuff'd bosom of that perilous grief
Which weighs upon the heart?"

Doct. "Therein the patient
Must minister unto himself."

Macb. "Throw physic to the dogs: I'll none of it."

Now, however, the victim of morbid fancies may be "ministered unto" in his otherwise hopeless affliction.

CASE OF C.—A man of forty-five years, hearty and strong, not in the least given to vain imaginings, but on the contrary decidedly practical in nature and material in his tendencies, complained of muscular rheumatism in the arms and back. The first attack came with a severe influenza cold, supposed to have been contracted by exposure in wet weather.

It was learned that shortly before the first attack, and during a cold storm, he—as an officer of the law, on duty in a public building—was attacked by a ruffian who had previously threatened his life, and was at that time creating a disturbance evidently with the purpose of carrying out the threat. The officer received a blow on the back from a heavy object, but succeeded in holding his ground and quelling the disturbance. The attack of influenza soon followed, leaving him with the painful feeling named rheumatism.

The causative mental action in this case was established in the following manner: During the moments of intense excitement, while injury was anticipated in a general way only, a mental picture of *general* fear of harm, perhaps worse, was formed without definite expectation. This feature of the mental agitation caused the influenza symptoms, which are a general inflammation of the mucous membrane and agitation of the entire system, with the aching that accompanies either the idea of severe muscular strain or the effect of repeated blows. The fear, which at first was only general, finally centered in one spot by means of the blow, which instantly concentrated all thought of injury at the point of impact. This final feature of the mental action caused the rheumatic pain in the back, which extended somewhat to other parts from the idea of a necessity for muscular exertion as a means of protection. All muscles that would naturally be called upon for protection under such circumstances shared the effects of the agitation established in mind.

The scene described was metaphysically treated without his knowledge that it was to be done, the request having been made by a member of his family and the treatment given in his absence, while the patient was, by material reckoning, nearly a thousand miles from the operator. Only the operator knew when the treatment was applied, neither did any one with the patient know certainly that the case was to be treated, no definite promise having been made. These facts exclude all possibility of any conscious act of imagination or of personal faith, on his own part or on the part of any one present with him, to determine the change in his condition. They also preclude the possibility of magnetic or electrical influence of a physical character between the personality of the operator and that of the subject. Yet, soon after the treatment was applied in New York, the pain disappeared from the body of the patient in a Western State, and the disease which was said to have been generated by exposure to cold and wet weather, vanished before a Thought-activity. No other possible reason save chance alone will intelligently account for this change. If it were an isolated case the question of chance might be entertained; but, in fact, it is only one among hundreds, differing in details, yet representing the same laws of Mental Action, and yielding to the same rules of application of the Universal Principles of human life. The writer holds voluntary letters from this patient acknowledging a complete cure, without apparent reason and with no personal knowledge that he was to be treated. Six years have elapsed since the above treatment, and there has never been the slightest return of the trouble. Facts are stranger than fiction; like Banquo's ghost, they "will not down."

CHAPTER XIII.

CURES THAT HAVE BEEN EFFECTED.
(Continued.)

Various Effects of Fright.

CASE OF D.—In 1886 this patient applied for mental treatment. He was then about forty years of age, and suffered with what appeared to be disease of the kidneys, which was pronounced by physicians to be well advanced. He was weak and pale, and lacked nervous vitality. Headache and severe pain in the lower part of the back were distinct features of the case. He had constantly declined under medical treatment, and was much discouraged at the time he decided to try metaphysical treatment.

A runaway accident that had occurred before the appearance of the first symptom, was the cause of his trouble. The principal features of the picture he had retained of the accident were as follows: While driving down a long hill, something broke in such a way as to throw him upon his back on the front of the wagon. In fact, he nearly went under the horse's heels. He was unable to hold the horse or, indeed, to do anything but keep himself from sliding off. The horse ran at will, kicking at nearly every leap. For a time he had no hope of escaping death, but finally extricated himself and escaped unharmed except by fright.

The mental picture formed during that period of terror continued sub-consciously in action; and the scene was continually re-enacted in the ganglionic nervous system, constantly generating disturbed action in the entire physical structure. If during the runaway he could have extricated himself sufficiently to regain control of his muscular system, he could have held the horse and danger would have been avoided. When he found this impossible, there was pictured in mind a lack of muscular power, developing the idea of Muscular Insufficiency. Later this idea was outwardly expressed in that physical condition known as "Muscular Degeneration," centered in the kidneys, because of circumstances rendering those vital organs intensely responsive at the time of the fright. When the picture of his own expected death by violent means was erased from his mind the ailment yielded immediately and he rapidly recovered. He was carefully watched for several years, but remained hearty and well with no sign of a return of the previous symptoms.

In cases of this order, both the intensity of mental action and its subtlety in developing physical correspondences are almost incomprehensible. Knowledge acquired by careful study of these modes of action is rare and priceless.

CASE OF E.—A gentleman of education, refinement and social advantages, had become intemperate in the use of alcohol. He had repeatedly declared that he would never again yield to temptation, and it was evident that he had made every effort to break off the habit, but without permanent success. In this state of mind he came to the writer for possible help, faithless, but despairing of other aid.

Tracing back the history of the case, the following facts were disclosed: He yielded to temptation, each time, after struggling with an attack of extreme nervousness which increased until he felt he could bear it no longer. Then he would drink, which temporarily quieted the agitation of the nervous system. When the nervousness reappeared, repeated drinks were resorted to until the nervous attack subsided.

It was learned that the nervous symptoms

appeared before the taste for liquor; and that the family physician gave him whiskey for relief, having no real remedy for the trouble. The alcohol and other ingredients in the whiskey, by poisoning the finer nerves, deadened the sensibilities for a time, thus affording *temporary* relief. In this manner the patient had learned to take a drink, instead of sending for the doctor who would resort to the same means when called. Thus the habit was acquired and grew.

Metaphysical philosophy shows that in all cases of this kind there exists a corresponding degree of mental agitation which is the direct cause of the nervous disturbance. Seeking for such a cause in this case, it was learned that before the first nervous attack the patient had been in a burning house surrounded by flames and, as it seemed, hopelessly cut off from escape. Death in a most horrible form seemed inevitable. He was rescued unharmed, though terribly frightened. Several spasms followed this fright; these grew less severe as time went on, until they were finally replaced by frequent and severe attacks of nervous agitation.

This experience was the original cause of his nervous attacks, and the habit was the outcome of the nervousness. In order to cure the habit the patient had to be relieved of the nervous condition. To relieve the nervousness, the mental agitation which caused it must be removed. To remove the mental agitation, the Mental Picture, which reacted upon the nervous system because of the persistence of the original thought of danger, must be rendered inoperative.

The cure was accomplished in the case described by a process of thought which obliterated the distressing agitation of the existing mental picture of death by flames—a danger which no longer existed. When this false idea was removed, its effect—the corresponding mental agitation—ceased. With the disappearance of the mental agitation, the nervousness also ceased, as no existing cause remained to perpetuate its action. When the nervousness failed to re-appear an appetite for something to quiet nervousness no longer existed—a human soul was freed from bondage and the man was cured! Three years have passed with no return of the desire for alcohol.

Many cases of inebriety arise from similar causes, varying greatly in detail but not in principle of action. Under the influence of these sub-conscious Mental Pictures, men are as powerless to cure themselves as though afflicted with neuralgia or rheumatism. Those who desire to discontinue the intemperate habit—provided they will co-operate with the Metaphysician in such ways as may be necessary to understand the facts in the case—can readily be cured by metaphysical treatment.

The Opium habit is frequently formed in the same way, and it is successfully treated by mental methods. Opium, instead of alcohol, is the medium employed to deaden sensibilities, but the reason for its use is the same, and the means of cure alike in both cases. Through its power to annihilate the disturbing mental picture which causes the nervous agitation, Metaphysical Healing is an adequate means of destroying both Intemperance and the Opium habit. To drug the human system into insensibility because the nervous system is unfortunately under a pressure of mental agitation, is unscientific and worse than useless. To erase from mind the agitating cause, in a harmless way, and thus put Nature again in control, is a method of procedure entirely reasonable and scientific.

There are numberless ways in which Mind, acting through rapid and intense thought under the manifold influences of fear, reacts upon the millions of nerves in the physical system to produce disease;

and a mental action rightly established in an opposite direction must inevitably result in a cure.

> "There are more things in heaven and earth, Horatio,
> Than are dreamt of in your philosophy."

CASE OF F.—This was a capable and energetic business man about forty-five years of age, troubled during a period of about thirty years with frequent, sudden and severe attacks of dysentery, and a constant tendency to inflammation of the bowels. When a lad he had suffered from repeated attacks of inflammation of the bowels, of a critical character. Later in life this derangement assumed the form of dysentery, accompanied by extreme nervousness, with intense excitement of the entire mental, nervous and physical mechanisms.

Before the first appearance of inflammation of the bowels he had been attacked by ferocious animals that followed him a long distance, compelling him to strain every nerve to the last degree of both speed and endurance. He escaped from them, but shortly thereafter was attacked by the illness that quite as nearly threatened to terminate his life as did the original incident.

The only cause of his frequent attacks of dysentery, through the period of thirty years, was that scene of terror, continually repeated in sub-conscious mental action, and reflected in a constant impulse to hurry. This impulse was expressed in every mental act of his life, and re-enacted in every nerve-throb of organic action. But for the fact that he possessed a naturally strong constitution, both mentally and physically, he must have succumbed to these attacks. In that event, the real cause of death, though unrecognized, would have been the original fright. Metaphysical treatment removed that element of fear from the aggregate mental action of his life's experience, and the physical system was relieved of its predisposing tendency to haste, and of the resulting indigestion in all its stages which had so often culminated in dysentery. Then the attacks ceased, and the system was gradually restored to healthy activity.

This man, with perfect confidence, had thoroughly tried every means known to medical practice, but experienced no permanent relief. Drugs only further taxed his nervous system without removing the cause of his trouble. The cause was mental, therefore only a Metaphysical process could reach it effectively. Others no doubt are in similar conditions because of the existence of like causes, and every such sufferer can readily be cured by a similar process of thought-action.

Many cases have come under the writer's notice where severe strain—mental, nervous and physical, under the influence of intense fear while in the act of flight from a source of danger—has so interfered with digestion and assimilation as to produce all degrees of mal-assimilation, indigestion, dyspepsia, diarrhœa, dysentery, inflammation of the bowels and even consumption of the bowels, which is the ultimate of all these lines of disturbed action.

The books of the medical schools give no information with regard to either the discovery or the removal of such causes of disease; therefore medical education does not enable one to perform a scientific cure in such cases.

CASE OF G.—Running in a state of intense mental excitement to a fire in plain sight, but at considerable distance, where the lives of loved ones were in danger, caused one of the most severe cases of chronic inflammation of the bowels ever recorded. This case, after many years' duration and several months of "heroic" medical treatment with opium, was pronounced hopeless by several medical men of high rank, acting in consultation. Yet it was entirely cured, years ago, by metaphysical treatment.

CASE OF H.—An especially severe case of insomnia, complicated with nervous dyspepsia, was caused by fright developed during the running away of a pair of horses which the man was driving. They ended by going over an embankment, with a complete smash-up, in which he expected to be killed. In fact, he stated that for the moment he THOUGHT *he had been killed*. This case was readily cured by metaphysical treatment. These symptoms may have different mental causes in other cases, but all result from distorted mental emotion, and the majority of them develop from some picture of fear which forms a mental image of injury or of death as the result of an accidental occurrence.

CASE OF I.—Eight years ago this patient, twenty-five years of age, applied for relief from an aggravated form of chills and fever. With full confidence in its power, medical treatment had been thoroughly tried, but had failed to cure. The patient was utterly faithless as regards the efficacy of mental influence in such a case, and frankly stated that he did not expect any benefit—he came only because urged by friends, and would remain only a sufficient time to prove that his case *could not be reached* by mental treatment. The chills were most violent, rendering him perfectly helpless for days at a time. He was employed at clerical work in a building located within a supposed malarious district. This was considered the reason for his condition.

Inquiry elicited the information that before this illness began he, with others, was sailing on Long Island Sound, several miles from land, when the boat ran on a rock which was just under water at ebb-tide. A storm was gathering and the waves ran high. There was no standing-place out of the boat, and there seemed to be no escape from drowning. After working for a long time in great fear, the boat was dislodged in a leaking condition and a landing for repairs was eventually made on an island. Here the patient had his first chill, and the attack was extremely violent. This attack was followed by others, similar in character, until he appeared for metaphysical treatment, which consisted in erasing the mental picture of death formed in his mind because of the apparently certain coming of that event. When this mental change was accomplished, the chills ceased immediately and entirely. The case was cured in a few weeks and, although he continued to live and work in the same so-called "malarious district," he had no recurrence of malarious symptoms.

If his disease was physical and the result of a physical cause, why did it vanish when only a mental change was made? This question has received no satisfactory answer through material reasoning, and it cannot be explained from any physical standpoint. The fact, however, stands out in bold relief, and cannot any longer be safely ignored.

This case, also, has been duplicated in many instances where some overpowering degree of fear was discovered to have preceded the first chill, and where all symptoms vanished when the picture of death or injury was erased from mind. Mental treatment properly applied is universally successful with similar cases. Scepticism as regards its efficacy can exist only because of ignorance of these facts.

Mental action in some form of fear underlies every case of chills;—usually the picture of death by some dreaded means is involved in the active cause. A general idea of danger of death, as a result of some particular condition supposed to be present in a certain locality, may sub-consciously spread from mind to mind through a community, by simple reflection of the mental picture of the Idea, causing an epidemic of "malaria," or other corresponding physical disease, to prevail. Remove that Idea from the general mind of that community, by any means whatever, and the prevalent disease will vanish, even though the material conditions of the locality remain unchanged.

This has been proved repeatedly in numerous localities. It is susceptible of proof in any locality at any time. Scepticism with regard to the theory will neither save those unfortunates who are subjected to such deleterious mental influences, nor prevent those who gain understanding of the laws of mental action, from reaping the reward in continued or restored health.

Publishers of newspapers, in their zeal to circulate what they are pleased to call news, are in many instances directly responsible for the spread of epidemics, by suggesting a special Image in the minds of their community. Speaking figuratively, it is equally possible for them to reverse the engine and thereby help to produce the opposite result. When this truth is recognized, a grave responsibility will be seen to rest upon those intrusted with constant access to the minds of a community.

Every thought has its accompanying Image, which in form, quality and character corresponds to the Idea entertained. While reading, persons form thought-pictures of the Ideas about which they read. These frequently become temporarily the dominant Ideas of life for each reader. The picture of the dominant Idea in mind multiplies in its reflections, extending to all receptive minds in a community. The trend of thought which prevails will show at least a coloring from that Idea.

Every thought, repeatedly indulged, leads eventually to corresponding actions in life's experience. Thought and action are inseparable.

The most powerful leader is he who places the highest and purest Ideas before the thinkers of a community.

Pure Ideals perpetuate pure thoughts, inevitably resulting in right actions. Purity and Health are co-existent.

CHAPTER XIV.

MUSCULAR AND INFLAMMATORY CONDITIONS.

Heart Disease, Fevers and Colds.

THE power of intelligence, as expressed in a process of thought working through the imaging faculty of mind to produce a corresponding physical condition, occupies a field of action so wide as to be almost incomprehensible: so deep in its sounding of human nature, and so weighty in its bearing upon the affairs of life as frequently to astound even the clearest thinkers—those most familiar with philosophical study. Common minds usually content themselves with a flat denial that any such power exists, without having taken the trouble to investigate. Scepticism, however, does not bring the question of the nature and cause of disease any nearer solution; neither does it in any respect dispose of the demonstrations continually being made—demonstrations which would be impossible if "*the mental imagery of an idea, and the physical reflection of its image,*" were not real principles of human life, in some important measure intelligently understood by their demonstrators.

As has been said, there are many particular ways in which the imaging faculty of mind is exercised through thought to cause disease in its manifold forms. Numbers of cases of muscular rheumatism have been traced directly to, and found to correspond exactly with the mental pictures of accidents—falls, runaways, and railroad or steamboat disasters.

The reason for this correspondence is that, at the moment of the occurrence, anticipation of physical injury prompts the mind to instantly place some or all of the muscles of the body under tension, more or less rigid, according to the intensity of the fear. This nearly universal impulse denotes a sub-conscious belief that muscular tension will tend to protect from injury. On the contrary, when the physical body is rigid under muscular tension at the moment of concussion, the injury is greater than if all muscles are relaxed, and in a natural state of flexibility.

The success of acrobats and tumblers in falling without injury depends upon knowledge of the safety in relaxed muscles during such movements.

The seemingly miraculous fact that infants or young children sometimes fall great distances and strike upon dangerous places, suffering little or no injury, is, perhaps, attributable to the circumstance that, not realizing danger, they are unconscious of fear, and the muscles are left free from tension at the moment of concussion.

Under rigid tension during fear, the body becomes more compact and inelastic, falls rapidly and strikes like a stone, thus rendering fracture almost certain. Under natural, fearless consciousness, the muscles remain flexible, and the body more expanded, in which condition it falls somewhat slower, striking more as would a soft substance, and thus receives less injury because offering less resistance. This is one reason—possibly the only one—why intoxicated persons frequently undergo falls and similar accidents, with less injury than others usually receive under similar circumstances; being in some degree unconscious of danger, muscular tension is not fully established.

In the majority of accidents, physical injury proceeds from, and corresponds to the state of resistance existing at the moment of concussion between the objects in collision. Reduce this resistance in any way and liability to injury will be proportionately lessened. The resistance of the human body will be either reduced or increased *to some extent* by the Mental State indulged at the time, whether it be conscious or sub-conscious.

Muscular tension, established at the time of an accident, frequently is renewed during a series of years, and some form of muscular or allied disease is almost certain to follow such continuance. In that event the disease has its origin in the muscular tension, which in turn results directly from the fear of injury. Remove from mind the continued sub-conscious remembrance of this fear and, with sufficient time for restoration of natural activity in the molecular construction, relaxation of the tense muscles must inevitably ensue. Every muscle of the body is equally subject to this line of action, both in causing and in curing disease.

Remember that the muscles are not separate things in themselves, capable of independent physical action, but that they all are under absolute control of the thinking mind, which uses them as submissive servants or as responsive instruments for either delicate or forcible action. The muscles do not command and the mind obey, but *vice versa*. Extend an arm. Now analyze this act: Did the arm physically extend itself, and then call upon you to observe its position? Did the muscles originate the intention and force the other tissues of the arm to reach forth, afterwards announcing to you their sovereign act of will? Or did *you* first mentally plan to extend *your* arm and then oblige the muscles to obey? Why does the arm remain in its rigid position? Because the mental action which caused it to stretch forth still continues. Close a finger on the palm of the hand; did not the mental intent precede the physical act? Cease the mental intent and the fixed tension of the muscles vanishes; repeat the intent and the tension recurs.

The marvelous rapidity of thought-action is an important feature which frequently leads to the erroneous conclusion that some muscular movements are involuntary, occurring because of physical impulse only. When any act is analyzed in all its phases, however, the necessity for both previous conscious intent and decisive act of the higher will, *either conscious or otherwise*, becomes apparent.

There is voluntary muscular action in response to mental volition, sub-conscious, conscious and super-conscious; through every degree of power—violent, strong, weak, feeble and faint, down to the almost imperceptible; but no *involuntary*, or purely muscular, action can ever take place. When mind *wholly* deserts the body the muscles *entirely* cease to move.

The physical body is an inanimate machine: Mind is its active centre, and Mental Action its only volition. Matter is void of intelligence.

Numerous cases of nervous prostration, resulting from surgical operations and the effects of ether, have been entirely cured in short periods of time by removing the mental impressions of those scenes, and the accompanying Idea of danger.

One particularly trying case, successfully treated, was that of a highly intelligent and capable young woman who had nervous prostration which culminated in acute melancholia. This disease progressed beyond the control of the family physician, who intended placing her in a public institution. The case was entirely cured, five years ago, by removing impressions of trying scenes connected with the death of dear ones. This person is now filling a public position of responsibility, and is in perfect health.

Several especially severe cases of congestion with pain at the base of the brain, have been permanently cured by removing the impression of fear produced by falls. In one instance the fall was backwards down stairs. In another it was backwards over a balustrade. Again, the fall was from a wagon which started without warning. In another instance, the person fell from a tree, striking on the back of the head and neck. All of these cases resulted in Basilar Congestion, because of the impression instantaneously photographed in mind of a critical danger located somewhere behind which, though unseen, was anticipated to the ultimate degree and realized as coming death. The *inaction* present in cases of congestion is a perfect physical picture of the idea of death.

Under such circumstances, as just described, an instantaneous demand—with more or less hopelessness, however—is made upon the Will for assistance; and the mental impression of fear is registered physically at the base of the brain and in the principal nerve centre of the spinal column, because that part of the nervous system corresponds most directly with the mental faculty of Will, responding immediately to its impulses. The details of accompanying symptoms vary somewhat with each case, because of the particular circumstances of the accident; but the principal results are alike.

Inflammation in all stages, from simple heat and irritation, to ulceration,—which is the ultimate action of inflammation,—has been traced with exactness to scenes of passion, excitement, fear or terror; where the imaging of heat, fire, flames, burning and consuming through inflammation, was the principal mental action involved, resulting either from accidents or from moral distortion.

When properly understood and intelligently traced, this theory applies to both external and internal heat and inflammation, of blood, muscles, nerves and organic structure; in neuralgia, rheumatism and fevers; in eruptive, ulcerative and suppurative diseases, and organic disturbances of all the physical organs. The correspondences are frequently so evident as to astonish one not familiar with this line of activity. The action is perfectly natural, however, and is at once intelligible, when it is understood that the *character* of a mental Image of a thought may be reproduced in the physical reflection of that thought. Fear reacts in heat, developing inflammation, which eventually results in ulceration and suppuration.

Serious cases of Eczema have been traced directly to scenes of fire, especially to great disasters—so-called "holocausts"—where the mental picture was formed from an Idea of the blistering, scorching and burning of human flesh. In the physical reflection each case exhibits the exact details of the particular picture formed in mind at the time of the occurrence. One picture will differ from another in minor points, but the general image is that of destruction from heat, or water and heat combined; and its physical copy will exhibit the same action, frequently reproducing the mental picture in the physical structure, even to the most minute detail of exact representation.

Some cases of this kind, the most hopeless on record, have been cured by removing mental impressions of horror arising from sympathy. The individual mind unaided is usually powerless to free itself from such a load of distorted emotion; with metaphysical assistance, however, it finally ceases to repeat the original action, when the physical copy fades and eventually disappears from the body. Correct application of metaphysical principles will cure every similar case.

Even to a novice, influenzas and colds frequently reveal the clearest possible correspondence with some recent mental excitement, varying in degree from simple anxiety down through the gamut of fear and fright to nervous shock. The most usual physical reflection of the mental emotion of fear, without reference to a definite picture of what was feared, is that which is commonly called *a cold*. This troublesome form of disease is inflammation of the mucous membrane, usually attended in some measure with constriction of the pores of the skin, thus shutting in the surplus heat that otherwise would escape. It is a state of feverish uneasiness, inflammatory in character, with every evidence of the element of fire or heat, instead of its absence—cold, in the system. The inflammation begins with molecular disturbance in the mucous membrane. This disturbance develops from nervous atomic vibrations, which in turn reflect from mental agitation in some degree of fear, or from mental emotion, as previously explained.

When suddenly frightened, or subjected to severe mental strain through sickness or death of friends, any person is likely to develop a cold, which will be either catarrhal, bronchial or pulmonary, or an influenza in some form, according to temperament and individual circumstances. The particular form of the cold is determined, not necessarily by what actually transpired, but rather by the particular Mental Picture which that mind forms of the occurrence, or of the features of anticipated danger.

In their first stages, many colds are influenzas, developing later into other forms. Such colds are invariably the effect of mental agitation established at the time either of an accident or of some other disturbing experience. These causes usually pass unrecognized, and the condition is nearly always attributed to some physical agency; but careful tracing, without prejudice, will bring to light a mental cause in every well-marked case.

The mental cause of a seeming cold may date back many years in the life of the patient, and may repeat its action from time to time, resulting in periodical colds or other attacks, perhaps at particular dates or seasons, or under certain corresponding circumstances which act as mental coincidences to re-establish the previous disturbed action. These conditions yield to right mental influence, and readily disappear under metaphysical treatment. Thousands of reliable witnesses testify to this fact, and it is being repeatedly proved in every day's practice.

Various forms of heart disease result from mental agitation attendant upon the death of relatives or friends. Grief and heart disease go hand in hand. The heart is the gauge of the emotions, and intense feeling registers there in direct proportion to the mental disturbance; the ultimate is instantaneous cessation of action of the heart, bringing this life-period to an end.

Cases are not uncommon in which a person, upon coming into the presence of the lifeless body of an especially dear friend, has fallen, and instantly passed away. Such changes are manifestly the outcome of mental emotion. Cessation of life is the result of nervous shock, which, in turn, is due to the mental image of death, self-centered at that moment in absolute degree. Acting under the influence of the mental picture of death, that Mind deserts its body. This manner of death is usually announced as the result of "heart disease." In many cases such a conclusion is little better than conjecture.

In those cases where a diseased physical condition was present it was the result of previous mental emotion in such lines of agitation as bear relation to the nature of the heart, and register there because of that relationship. This previous disturbance left the individual with a mental picture which established a predisposition to excitement from similar mental influence; the result—sudden death—was all the more probable because of that mental reason.

While Materia Medica has no remedy for such a mental state, and medical science can only surmise the cause of illness previous to the autopsy, Metaphysical Healing goes to the root of the matter at once by discovering and removing the original predisposing mental disturbance which has been constantly weakening the heart's action and generating disease in its tissues. This restores all organs and functions to their normal condition, after which, predisposition to attacks of "heart failure" disappears, and the Individual, if called upon to go through an ordeal, will have sufficient natural strength to undergo the trial without disaster.

When mind thinks, each vital organ responds in a corresponding degree of activity, regardless of conscious recognition of the fact by the individual. On both the sub-conscious and the super-conscious planes of mental action, the heart is under absolute control of mind through Thought-action: it instantly responds to and accurately registers mental emotion in the direction of either death or life.

The thought of death means Departure from life on this particular plane of existence. The thought of Life, fully realized in mind, means healthy, living activity on all planes.

The real man of spiritual essence, the intelligent Individual having actual Being, is life eternal—a living entity of indestructible Reality. No deathly element could ever have mingled with the ingredients of his constitution, because living activity—Life—is the only absolute reality in the Universe, and with life once realized no different reality remained to be acquired. If death had entered before realization of life, then life would have been of no avail, for death already held the portal. Life and death can never occupy together. Life cannot die; Death cannot live. That which does not live can never act. Life is a deathless reality; Death but a lifeless illusion. Man never dies—he only changes his field of conscious action, or enters on another plane of life's experience. Traveling round the circumference of the wheel of active Being, he perhaps inadvertently slips back on one of its spokes, returning to the centre from which he sprang; then, gathering fresh impetus, he again springs forward, once more to realize the outermost action of the circumference, in Individual experience. Thus his life progresses in periods of seeming separateness with an end to each interval; but the wheel goes perpetually onward in the harmonious activity of eternal life, and man travels with the wheel, having no conscious choice in the matter.

The impulse of Eternal Life is irresistible.

CHAPTER XV.

THE COMMON GROUND OF HEALING METHODS.

Why do Conflicting Theories Heal?

IF the theory that a mental picture is the cause of sickness be true, why is it that those who pay no conscious attention to these pictures, even in mental practice, but believe quite differently with regard to the nature and cause of disease, also produce cures?

This important point should be lucidly explained. All evidence established during accurate examination of the subject, invariably goes to support the theory that the Imaging faculty of mind is involved in every cause and in every cure of disease, regardless of the external means employed.

In the first place, every case of disease yet brought forward for examination in metaphysical practice, has exhibited well established mental impressions, or pictures in mind, that bear direct correspondence to the disease, in character, quality and form.

In the second place, many people have thoroughly tried all other methods of cure, including those of the various mental schools, without permanent help. Yet, on the discovery and removal from mind of corresponding pictures, they have recovered, sometimes almost immediately.

Many schools of practice exist in all parts of the world, varying in theory from extremely material views to the highest spiritual ideas. Each of these schools produces cures. All cannot be entirely correct in theory unless the Life and Being of man is a most discordant mixture, with no sure foundation —illogical, inconsistent and unreal. Neither philosophy nor science points to such a conclusion.

The fact that all schools produce cures, suggests that there may be a common Law of Activity, capable of being called into action without full consciousness of the process, which action, if established, will result in a cure regardless of the means employed. If so, that Law is discoverable, and when fully comprehended will prove universal in application.

Some people recover while taking medicine; and the cure seems to have been effected by direct action of the medicine itself. This usually adds strength to the opinion that the disease was an actual physical thing, and that the medicine prescribed was the particular ingredient which Nature intended as a remedy for that disease. This opinion is frequently entertained regardless of the fact that the list of *remedies* named by the schools as Nature's real curative substances is changed every two or three decades—in fact, is constantly changing.

While one person takes medicine and recovers, another, equally sick in the same way, turns to the Faith Cure, and recovers without any physical application of the so-called *nature's remedy*. Another prays by himself, without the aid of a special organization; he also recovers with no other sensible means than his own effort to attract the attention of a healing power. Others perform some ceremonious act; wear an amulet, or carry a souvenir—perhaps a horse-chestnut in the pocket, or a bean, or a stone. All of these methods produce cures to prove their efficiency. No one, however, explains these results satisfactorily to those who are inclined to think and to investigate for the sake of knowledge. Why is it possible to obtain approximately the same result through widely different means?

While some are cured by faith, others go unrelieved in spite of the same agency. This, also, may truly be asserted of Medicine in all of its schools and branches. Why is it that all schools heal some cases, while none of them succeed with all curable cases of any given malady?

The following tenets of theory are believed to be indisputable :

1. If there is but one true theory with regard to the cause and development of disease, then there can be but one true principle of cure.

2. If there exists only one true way to heal the sick, then all methods differing from that one must be developed from false theories through mistaken ideas.

3. A false theory contains no power for the direct healing of disease, because falsity is devoid of principle, and without principle there can be no law, consequently no power for action.

4. If the real cause of disease is many-sided, so that sickness comes through channels bearing no direct relation to one another, then no single line of action and no one means of cure can reasonably be expected to apply in all cases. In that event no school, confining its efforts to one principle of cure, has exclusive right to the treatment of disease.

5. Disease may be many in its particulars, yet only

one in its nature; in which case the *true Theory* of cause as well as of cure must be the same for all forms of sickness; each separate kind being a part only of the one nature, and each particular application a mode of employing the one healing power.

The facts underlying these tenets may be concentrated as follows:

If there be one fundamental Character to all disease, there also must be one fundamental Cause, of which local causes are only branches. In that event, one theory of cure will be the foundation of all true curative influence.

Examine, for a moment, the apparent facts in the various methods of treatment and their common results:

Under analysis, the different schools of practice resolve into two common classes: On the one hand, those holding that disease is physical, and of the body only, and following a theory of herb, drug or chemical medication; and on the other, those believing disease to be a condition of the mind and susceptible of mental cure. There are branches to each of these schools which deviate from the pure theories and somewhat confuse methods, but the main idea of each school with regard to the nature, cause and cure of sickness is adhered to by each branch. It is indisputable that both these schools perform cures in all their branches; therefore, curative action is not confined to any one school, method or means. The vital question is, *How* is the cure performed? Is it physical in one case and mental in the other? If so, then both mind and matter have independent power for action. Is there any common ground on which advocates of both these theories can meet, examine facts, and prove that both produce results through the same laws?

When rightly studied, one common element is found in every form of disease, namely: Discordant Action. Without this no disease can develop. It seems certain, therefore, that there must exist one line of activity for all causes of disease—a line which corresponds to the discordant action involved. This must be either physical or mental; it can not be both, and still be only one activity. No activity can operate on other than its own plane; therefore, both the cause and cure of any disease must be of the same order.

Are all these cures physical? Emphatically no! Those wrought in the various mental schools are mainly in cases where no physical remedies were employed. To state that because the patient recovered without medicines, it is proved there was nothing the matter, is to confess complete ignorance of mental action and its established facts. In the physician's case, it frequently means refuting his own diagnosis—sometimes a diagnosis based upon consultation with eminent authorities.

Are all cures performed mentally? At first thought this also seems impossible, for in many cases medicines were administered under medical treatment and the patients recovered.

During impartial examination of the subject, one important fact always appears: While in many cases treated mentally no physical means were employed, and there was no material agency to which the cure could possibly be attributed, yet in every case treated physically, the factors of mind and mental action were undeniably present in some important degree. The physician had hope, and confidence in his own ability. The patient also had hope and probably considerable confidence, with growing expectation which finally reached the point of *mental realization* of a cure—a most potent factor. Others, perhaps, took part in this super-conscious mental action, thus contributing to the aggregate of courage, confidence, hope and realization of recovery. In all ages and among all classes of people instances have been recorded where a mother has held out against the most decided assurance of the physician that her child was sick unto death, and that no human power could save its life; and by sheer force of mental determination she has held its little life above and safe from the mental danger which then overshadowed it because of false beliefs with regard to the supposed fatal powers of disease. Every such victory demonstrates beyond question that a power rests in mind which can overthrow disease and conquer death, even on the plane of determined will—by no means the most powerful plane of mental action. Why should not mankind have the full benefit of knowledge pertaining to that power? In all similar cases, the body is controlled by mind, each mind assisting the other, perhaps not consciously, but with effective results. If no one, either present or absent, has any hope, confidence or realization of life and health, and if no correct mental action be established on any of the three planes of consciousness, material science proves of no avail.

With the larger number of cases treated successfully by mental methods, physical means of cure is out of the question, and mental activity is the only factor involved; while in medical treatment there invariably is mental action as well as physical means, and both appear as possible factors in the cure, until each is adequately examined.

It is a well-known fact that where no mental

action is involved, medicine does not operate. No physician would attempt to medicate a lifeless body. Life must be present, with mind active in some degree, on some one of the *three planes of consciousness*, or no effect can be produced by medicine. Without life there is no action; without consciousness there is no life, and without mind there is no consciousness on this plane of living action.

When these facts are carefully weighed, it seems reasonable to suppose that the mental plane of action, which is invariably involved in every case of either a cause or a cure, may be the plane on which the curative act is *always* performed. If this be so it follows that in all methods, excepting the purely mental, which relies upon no other means, the cure must have been effected through a mental action established without conscious recognition.

This we claim is the underlying fact of all methods of cure—Medical, Chemical and Electrical;—by Water, Rest, Travel, Change, Massage, Color, Music, Prayer, Faith or Superstition. With each a mental factor is sub-consciously involved in the operation, and *if for any reason that action is not established*, there is no cure in that case.

The faith-healer of the Church will not attempt a cure unless the patient on his own account has faith that the Supreme Being is about to perform a special act for his good. This is distinctly a mental act of realization of a cure. The competent physician is reluctant, and may even refuse, to treat a patient who doubts his ability, or lacks sufficient confidence to establish what is really a mental realization of a cure in his own case; thus, perhaps unconsciously, demanding faith as imperatively as does the faith-curist. If the disease be purely physical, and the medicines are the true remedies, possessing independent power for direct action on the disease itself, regardless of mental action, why should any degree of faith or confidence be necessary or even an important factor?

In every case of this kind the patient is thrown upon his own responsibility to cure himself. The external means operate advantageously only because they serve as a medium to arouse the required amount of confidence. Both mental and physical schools fail with many cases where cures would be effected if the real laws involved in both cause and cure were sufficiently understood by their practitioners.

The teachings of all Schools of Mental Healing train students in the application of thought to a given purpose, along lines which result in a change of the dominant Idea, and the change is from that which generates a picture of discord to such as will inevitably result in harmony and health. This mental change may be effected by the thought of another, regardless of conscious thought on the part of the patient; in which event a cure is effected not only independent of his faith in it, but even against extreme incredulity. This fact has repeatedly been proved in the cases of persons who, through avowed scepticism, refused treatment, yet were treated and permanently cured without their own knowledge or consent; also in the cases of children and others, not responsible for their own decisions, and with the demented, who could not be reasoned with about their condition. These facts are now of daily occurrence.

Mental pictures capable of causing disease may be formed by any wrong process of thought. The moral plane of action contains important factors of this sort. Recognizing this, some advocates of Mental Healing erroneously attribute *all* sickness to direct sinful act.

Whatever thought forms a picture not in accordance with the real laws of life, becomes the cause of some degree of sickness which will come to the surface in due time. Immoral thoughts, as surely as accidental happenings, form erroneous pictures, which establish discordant modes of action. In either event, the most effectual application of principle through thought, is such as will enable the operator to discover the particular picture formed in that mind, and to change the mental action to a better mode by placing higher objects before the understanding. This not only cures the disease, but brings about the needful reform. This result can be accomplished only through the Imaging faculty of Mind, and with universal success, only through the highest act of Imagination—the Imaging of real Ideas.

If those mental healers, of any school, who suppose that they produce results independent of mental pictures, will closely examine their method of procedure in applying mental treatment, it will become apparent that the process of thought which comprises treatment, whether it be a continued train or an instantaneous flash of thought-activity, operates through the Imagination, in Mental Imagery, and produces the desired result only by changing action in the patient's mind, thereby removing a picture of disturbing nature and substituting one that is harmonious in character.

The activities of mind are so subtle that these pictures frequently are changed super-consciously, without either party concerned being aware of the circumstance.

While some thought-activities are slow in their

procedure, others result in an instantaneous change of mental pictures. Without a mental picture there can be no thinking process, and without a change of mental picture there can be no change of thought. Therefore, if no mental picture be either removed or replaced, no cure will be effected. There can be no deviation from this universal law of mental action in the life of individuals.

Some people are ill because pictures of wrong thoughts have been harbored until false action has become temporarily established. Any process of thought, whether instantaneous or continued, sufficient to eradicate that wrong mental action and establish a right mode instead, will cure that case. In the case of others, the sickness is caused by particular mental pictures of injury, of death, or some form of fear not necessarily associated with immoral actions. These cases can be cured permanently only by erasing the particular pictures which caused the special symptoms.

Treating solely along moral lines, on the theory that only sin causes sickness, will never efface a picture of fright; and although treatment applied, on general principles, might act to modify mental action, and thereby render temporary relief, still there is a feature of chance in the attempt, and the ultimate result is decidedly uncertain. But the process of erasing the particular picture of discord, whether it be generated by immorality in sinful thought, by fright, or by the two combined, must invariably result in a permanent cure—and this regardless of direct faith or expectation on the part of either patient or operator. Through such application of principles every curable case may be reached understandingly, leaving nothing either to chance action or subconscious influence.

Neither the range of thought nor the scope of power are in any way limited by giving attention to the special cause. In reality, both are thereby extended; because, by understanding the laws involved in every mode of mental action, direct thought can be applied to all kinds of cases throughout the entire range of mental and spiritual activities. Thus the metaphysician is prepared to deal intelligently with every vicissitude of life.

The deepest principles of Divine Reality are outwardly expressed in the living activities of the intelligence of Man. These activities are consciously exercised, and can be intelligently studied only through the Imaging faculty which, on its various planes of action, enables Man to come in contact with all things real. On the lowest and most outward plane of life the Imaging faculty enables one to recognize forms and objects of sense. On the next higher and more inward plane, through the same faculty, the living soul recognizes laws of action and their accompanying results. On the highest plane, Divine Intelligence, shining through the spiritual nature of the Individual, illumines every faculty, making possible the recognition of principles through *pure imaging of real Ideas*. Perfect exercise of the Imaging faculty, therefore, will develop the best modes of action in every stage of progress, and eventually lead to the highest conceptions possible to the human mind, culminating in purest spiritual perceptions of fundamental truths. This is an attainment possible for every intelligent individual. The value of the means leading to so high an end cannot be overestimated.

Knowledge of the Universe is within the grasp of every one who learns to properly exercise this wonderful faculty, for within human comprehension there exists no limit to its action.

One who ignores Universal Law thereby limits his powers and, sub-consciously, confines his efforts within narrow bounds; while he who recognizes the law, and conforms to it in every instance, searching for and obliterating the harmful picture in each case, succeeds with all classes. The scientific application of curative mental influence lies entirely in this direction.

The Principles of Being are involved in every moral question, and are expressed in all the laws of active life. These laws are the instruments which must be employed in conscious thought to produce right results. When thoroughly understood, all laws of life are recognized in the Unity of the one Principle of Being. ONE is the Principle and the Law of all Reality, and one Law applies to all.

In Eternal Principle all things are whole.

CHAPTER XVI.

CONCLUSION.

The Importance of the Movement.

THE necessarily limited scope of this work will not admit of extended consideration of the subject of Metaphysical Healing through all its interesting and instructive phases. Enough, perhaps, has been said to explain the general ground of the philosophy of thought involved, and to illustrate the practical application of metaphysical principles to the healing of disease—which is all that has been attempted.

This work is not intended as an argumentative treatise, but rather it is a necessarily limited presentation of a subject of great depth, containing knowledge of which humanity is in urgent need. The cases cited in the preceding chapters are not intended as *proofs* to those who have had no similar experience, but simply as illustrations of the modes of action through which results are obtainable.

Similar illustrations any intelligent individual may trace out for himself in the experiences of those around him. Marked exemplifications of the fact that a given case of sickness was preceded by a mental disturbance closely resembling the abnormal physical condition, will frequently be met with in such investigations. Careful study of the subject will prove to each inquirer what the illustrations given here prove only to those who were interested in their development.

These are by no means either the most remarkable correspondences between cause and effect, or the best results in healing that have been effected. Many who read these pages will recall cases of a more marked character which have been permanently cured. Those here presented have been selected with a view to a clear tracing, in lines which can easily be followed by those unfamiliar with the theory, and also as cases showing a single symptom resting upon a single cause, because such afford plainer examples of the working of the laws. Complicated cases which usually exhibit more wonderful phases of mental action have been excluded, because they are more difficult to understand. There is, however, a superabundance of such cases on record, and they clearly illustrate almost every phase of mental activity in its relationship to physical action. In every case of the kind thus far treated, the following facts have been conclusively established:

1st. The particular mental picture, which by reflection produced the physical symptom, was not formed until its causative Image of fear or emotion entered the activity of that mind. The action proceeds as follows:

(a) The Image of fear of personal harm, first formed in mind.

(b) The Picture of the exact details of the anticipated injury.

At this point the *general* Image and the *special* Picture merge into one form of mental activity, and, uniting in reflected physical action, they become the direct Cause of the Disease eventually generated by that action.

2d. The Disease did not appear until after the corresponding Mental Picture was definitely formed; sometimes not until years had elapsed.

3d. The disturbance continued with more or less intensity until the Image of fear was identified and its element of discord mentally removed.

The circumstances of life sometimes cause an Image to lie dormant in mind, and its physical reflection to remain practically inactive for a time, but it is likely to be aroused at any moment by a predisposing circumstance. The individual is never safe until this Image has been removed. As soon as the Image is erased the disease begins to yield, and it finally disappears altogether, with greater or less rapidity, according to the individual circumstances of the case. Some conditions require hours, and some days; while other cases, equally curable, require weeks or months for natural mental action to become fully expressed in thoroughly rejuvenated physical tissue throughout the entire system. If the right mental action be established and continued, however, a natural healthy physical condition must eventually result.

The facts of cure expressed in these cases are considered as evidence of the existence of definite laws which, for the good of humanity, should be studied until they can be universally applied. It is idle to attempt to put them aside with the plea that "what has been, is good enough for us." The human family is overburdened with fear and disease. The former can not be dealt with medically; the latter assumes many hitherto incurable forms, because of which men live in terror and die in anguish.

The application of thought to a given case for a definite purpose, with intelligent understanding of certain laws of activity which underlie that particular case, has already been proved a power for good, without the possibility of harmful complications. Mental Healing, therefore, is a blessing to suffering humanity. For these reasons its advent is hailed with joy by those who wish to see humanity benefited, and every intelligent thinker who comes rightly into its understanding must in some measure recognize its importance. The greater the intelligence, the more prompt and responsive the recognition.

"Metaphysics"—The Science of the Real Life of Being—is already well established as the true philosophy of life, and is bound to gain ground even more rapidly as its principles become better known. Its healing efficiency will also increase in power and scope as knowlege of the application of thought to the manifold experiences of life becomes extended. With time for suitable growth of understanding, through extended research and universal demonstration, this knowledge will raze from the field of human life that monstrous structure of physical disease, with its thousands of terrifying names—all devised in the schools. Then may we calmly view the merry dance of joy held over the remains of the last school which teaches that man is mainly a chemical receptacle, and that the only way to reach the inner recesses of his being with a remedy is through his mouth, while the only element that can "scientifically" give him health and extend the period of his life, is some vile ingredient possessing only deadly qualities. "Life" brought to man in the vessel of death frequently proves to be but the dregs from the cup of the unwelcome messenger. A deadly drug contains no life: the belief that it does is a fatal illusion.

The facts of Metaphysical understanding do not rest upon statement alone; they can be intelligently examined by means of results which are of daily occurrence, and are constantly increasing both in number and in scope, and any individual who enters upon the examination will find himself in a numerous and thoroughly respectable company.

It is claimed that Metaphysical Healing is a right and reasonable means of relieving suffering humanity of its burden of medically incurable diseases, and it is hoped that the facts here presented may lead to careful individual investigation. Unprejudiced inquiry certainly will prove the justice of the claim.

No one is expected to believe, simply because it is asserted, any statement which from his standpoint seems unreasonable; but each is asked to suspend judgment until opportunity is found for adequate examination of the subject, and then to examine impartially for his own sake and that of those dear to him. Under intelligent scrutiny, facts will be disclosed and truth realized for permanent good. The only Elixir for the perfect healing of the nations lies in a pure understanding and a right application of Metaphysical Principles, which belong to everybody and are free to all. They are never written upon a sheepskin; simply *to understand* is the only diploma required for either authority or power.

Believing or disbelieving either what others say, or what at first thought seems right or wrong from one's own point of view, will not necessarily result in the acquirement of knowledge of real Truth. Only patient, painstaking examination of the subject, without fixed preconceived opinions on the Ideas to be dealt with, can reveal the actual facts. Through idle argument alone no one can be rightly convinced. Proofs rest within individual comprehension, and must be acquired at the fountain-head.

In lines of action similar to those explained in the previous chapters, *Discordant mental emotion underlies every known disease.* Though at first sight many of the modes are intricate, and difficult for the untrained mind to conceive, yet they are clearly explainable.

All the knowledge acquired from the books and professors of all the Medical Schools in the world leaves the student still ignorant of this vital pathological fact. .The deepest learning and the greatest skill, derived from the experiences of a lifetime spent with the numerous sciences included in a medical education, leave their professor still helpless as an infant to deal with these mental causes of disease. Yet, every practicing physician is constantly surrounded with cases parallel to these, and every patient who appeals for aid is suffering from some picture of distress, which would readily yield to mental influence, rightly applied at the real seat of the trouble.

This explains the fact that so many cases classed as hopeless are found upon the list of every prominent medical practitioner. Such cases are readily cured by any one possessing sufficient knowledge of the laws involved in Mental Causes to obtain a correct mental diagnosis and to give adequate mental treatment based upon real metaphysical principles. Detailed knowledge of the physical body and of so-called physical disease is no more necessary to the effectual performance of such a cure than detailed knowledge of brush-making is necessary to the portrait painter.

The results already accomplished can no longer be denied while we retain the capacity for intelligent recognition of facts in the Universe, neither can they be explained under the laws of the physical sciences;

therefore they demand, and in time will receive, due attention from scientific thinkers. The Metaphysical then will be recognized as the true platform of the Physical, where all thinkers may stand, and think, and work in unison for the good of all, for the truth in all, and for the eternal right that inheres in every living atom of the boundless Universe of Reality.

All the minds of living men combined do not yet know all that is taking place in the universe or on this earth—not even in a grain of sand, much less in the intricate affairs of human life.

Unyielding prejudice is a millstone hanging about the neck of the modern materialist, and he is bound to go down with it unless he cuts loose through free investigation of facts. Truth can not be strangled, and facts will not remain underground.

The one eternal fact of existence is the progressive action of real life, a perpetually revolving wheel of active law, at every turn of which fresh facts are brought to the surface, exposing to view principles of value to every individual. If we are withstanding the eternal advancement of Universal Law, we must expect to be engulfed in the spiritual wave of progress which is now surging through the soul of intelligent man, cleansing his faculties of every obstructive influence and purifying every purpose.

Life is action, and action is progress. He who ceases to progress, ceases action, eventually crystallizes, and physically ceases to live.

Definite Law is expressed in every real activity, and Principle underlies every law. Through reasonable analysis of Ideas, based upon intelligent understanding, both Principle and Law are accessible to every individual.

Intelligent Understanding is a genuine faculty inherent in the spiritual nature of every human being. Through conscious thought, based upon correct understanding of first principles, any desirable right action may be established by any thinker. When such truth is called into activity by one mind, its unfolding harmonies radiate and spread unrestrained throughout the extent of Universal Mind, eventually leading millions into the field of Intelligent Understanding of Principles, where every spring bubbles over with the health which sparkles in its depth, and every rill dances in the eternal joy of living action.

Thought, is an active spiritual power:
Man, its living master.

THE END.

Printed in New York.

New Light
FROM THE
Great Pyramid!

THE ASTRONOMICO-GEOGRAPHICAL SYSTEM OF THE ANCIENTS RECOVERED AND APPLIED TO THE ELUCIDATION OF HISTORY, CEREMONY, SYMBOLISM AND RELIGION.

By ALBERT ROSS PARSONS.

Whenever we hear of growls from the Russian Bear, or of the American Eagle flapping his wings, we recognize at once the familiar heraldic emblems of the Russian Empire and the American Republic. In the present work it is shown for the first time that the only bears set in the stars fall to Russia, and the only eagles to America, by virtue of a prehistoric universal astronomico-geographical system, which also displays the constellation Taurus over the Taurus mountains, and the ancient Chersovesus Taurica (the modern Crimea), which was the home of the Tauric, or bulls, the Scythian ancestors of the modern Saxons, or people known as John Bull ; and in like manner the constellation Perseus over Persia ; Orion over Iran ; Medusa over the Medes ; the Unicorn over British India ; Capricornus-Pan over Panama ; the Ram over Rome ; the flaming Lion and Dragon over China ; Cygnus-Canaan over Canada ; Virgo over the Pacific Ocean (the Blessed Virgin, and Star of the Sea being known in the Orient not as Virgo, but as Dhurga), etc.

The work contains maps both of the surface of the Globe and of the constellations in the Heavens, with numerous rare and significant illustrations of great value.

NEW LIGHT FROM THE GREAT PYRAMID is copiously illustrated, handsomely printed, and bound in a substantial manner, scientific size, and is a most important addition to the literature of the day.

PRICE, $4.00.
Postpaid to any part of the World reached by the Postal Union.

THE TRADE SUPPLIED.

PUBLISHED BY
THE METAPHYSICAL PUBLISHING CO.
331 Madison Avenue, New York.

PARSIFAL

THE FINDING OF CHRIST THROUGH ART

A Wagner Study

By Albert Ross Parsons

Extracts from Private Letters to the Author.

From an Episcopal Clergyman.—"I have read closely and with deep interest your 'Wagner Study.' In a purely literary sense you have done your work admirably; but this is only incidental to your purpose, which is one of grave moment in these times, when such crowds of thoughtless but apparently cultured people are making an idol of Wagner without knowing why, or indeed at all understanding the religious and ethical source from which sprang the noble and characteristic inspiration of his masterful genius. To me the massive and luminous quality of Wagner's handling of the fundamental truths of Christianity is of the nature of a revelation. The depth and grasp of his mind were remarkable, and joined to these there is an air of profound sincerity which gives added weight and charm to his thoughts. I hope your essay may have a wide circulation."

From a Surgeon and Author.—"No one can read until he appreciates the full import of Wagner's utterances, without perceiving that in his own way he had gained a vision of the Redeemer which the intellectual eye alone never can. In its analytical range our mental sight is even more limited than the physical eye, which sees only a portion of the field of the spectrum and, therefore, has to learn by other means that there are powerful rays at either end which are wholly invisible to it. But Wagner's testimony is of the highest value for one reason, namely, that art owns birth of spirit rather than of mind, of heart more than of intellect, and it was therefore by deep, true feeling that Wagner found the unsatisfactoriness of every voice in this world that was not Christ's. He did so because he felt so much, and thus passed beyond the narrow range of purely intellectual light, to the other light which is also power."

From the President of a Branch of the Theosophical Society.—"When your charming book reached me, I was just starting for A—. I took it with me and enjoyed it very much. It has gone into other hands and I think is to make quite a circuit. So you see the good work goes on. Probably we are sowing, you and I, different kinds of grain, but I think it is grain although there may be some tares among it."

From a Clergyman.—"I cannot tell you adequately how I have enjoyed your noble exposition, and I cannot overstate my appreciation of it."

From a Clergyman.—"I have taken great pleasure in your unveiling of the religious thoughts of the musical poet and seer of these late days—his baton a divining rod! There is none but must consider how great this man was, who calls forth such an army of loving interpreters, and who from whatever side he is viewed so enforces admiration. I thank you for the thoroughness of your work and the valuable suggestions and side lights of your own thought."

From a College Professor and Author.—"I do not know that I ever read a work which so satisfied me as does your 'Parsifal,' and I cannot but appreciate not only its literary merit, but its artistic and ideal realization. It comes as near to my idea of a book as possible. The body full and to the point, and self-clothed with enough out of its great topic to need no more; and the appendices so copious that they are an argument in themselves, and a firm foundation for whatever in the text seemed to call for them. I took a real and positive pleasure in the reading of it."

From a Clergyman and Author.—"Your synopsis of Wagner's writings on theology has been an entire feast for me, while your appendices do notably support both his and my own work."

From a Clergyman and Author.—"I have read Mr. Parsons' interesting 'Parsifal' with sincere interest and admiration. Mr. Parsons has shown a marked spirit of reverence, and his critical discrimination is singularly acute and felicitous."

Notices of the Press.

"Mr. Parsons has been long and favorably known as one of the leading musicians of America, but it is a matter of no little surprise to find him possessed of so thorough a theological equipment. Evidently philosophy has been the intellectual relaxation of his otherwise busy life. By the creation of 'Parsifal' Wagner is shown to the world as the exciter of the deepest religious emotion, a guide to spiritual heights through new paths, a modern reviver of the *extasis* of the Neo-Platonists, through the unconditioned power of music."—*Home Journal*, New York.

"Mr. Parsons has been a wide reader and a deep thinker. His studies in Wagner at first hand have enabled him to give a remarkable interpretation to the theological significance of the great German master. Among the signs of the times, few are more striking to the thoughtful observer than the fact brought out by this volume, that the man who confessedly stands at the head of modern music, and who has been popularly supposed to represent the Pagan Renaissance, did in reality travel the historic road by which humanity climbed out of Paganism into Christianity, and made his rich and noble art a veritable finding of Christ. When the priest and the doctor have done with their ecclesiastic and theologic talk, and the world still holds aloof, it may be for the artist and the poet, the philosopher and the musician, to lift aside the veil hiding the real Christ and show him unto men, pointing out the real meaning and value of our symbols of worship and of faith."—*All Souls Monthly*.

"A thoughtful work on Wagner's last masterpiece 'Parsifal,' showing great sympathy with the composer's intentions."—*Detroit Free Press.*

"A very full and enthusiastic exposition of the views Wagner held at the close of his life as to the reality and power of Christ's relations to men. A valuable appendix contains much additional matter."—*Public Opinion*, Washington.

"Many will be amazed at the new Wagner Mr. Parsons presents to us, although it is a Wagner accessible to all of us in his collected writings. It cannot be denied after reading Mr. Parsons' more than interesting volume, that Wagner was a profound thinker on Christianity."—*Musical Courier*, New York.

"Mr. Parsons' clever and stimulating essay on 'Parsifal' will repay perusal."—*The Churchman*, New York.

"It has evidently been a labor of love to present Wagner in this way, and the work deserves respect. It is published with an appendix which is even larger than the body of the text, but it is all well worth reading and ought to make Wagner even more popular than ever before."—*Boston Post*.

"A profoundly interesting and instructive writing, and in a comparatively new field."—*Portland Oregonian*.

"These utterances of Wagner are quite original, and the citations are cleverly arranged to show the progressive steps by which he reached an understanding of the Light of the World. 'Parsifal' will reward attentive perusal."—*Philadelphia Ledger*.

"Those to whom Wagner's music brings uplifting, spiritual thoughts, will deeply rejoice in this earnest, loving presentation of the words of a great man."—*New Haven Palladium*.

"An addition of an unusual kind to the multitudinous Wagner literature. Wagner has been presented to us in many shapes. Here he is shown as a theologian, and Mr. Parsons' ingenuity and analysis will no doubt be appreciated. The earnest and moving words used by Mr. Parsons seem entirely justified. It is altogether a very suggestive and interesting record."—*Philadelphia Telegraph*.

"Those to whom the name of Wagner stands only as the symbol of music, cannot fail to be surprised and pleased at the depth and range of his philosophical thinking, many examples of which are here presented. The universal disease of society is want of brotherly love—it is not the great deeds, but the sufferings of men, that bring us near to them."—*Werner's Magazine*.

Second Edition—Cloth, $1.25.

Postpaid to any part of the World reached by the Postal Union.

PUBLISHED ONLY BY

THE METAPHYSICAL PUBLISHING COMPANY,

331 MADISON AVENUE, NEW YORK.

THE Philosophy of Mental Healing.

By LEANDER EDMUND WHIPPLE.

This book contains a clear interpretation of the scientific status of the Mental Healing movement, based upon extended practical experience in successful demonstration.

The work is the result of careful study and exhaustive research along mental lines, and is replete with valuable information not to be found in any other printed work, including a variety of illustrations of cures effected by mental means.

It treats in a thoroughly practical manner of such subjects as Metaphysics *versus* Hypnotism, Mental Healing and Surgery, Telepathy, Thought Images, the Effects of Fright, Mental Causes, Curative Influences, the Law of Correspondences, and other equally important subjects, and is intensely interesting from beginning to end.

This work stands alone in scientific exposition of the facts of Metaphysical Healing, thus occupying independent ground in the literature of to-day. It is indispensable to every well-informed person and an acquisition to every library.

Elegantly printed on fine paper. Handsomely bound in cloth and gold.

PRICE, $2.50

Postpaid to any part of the world reached by the Postal Union.

The trade supplied.

THE METAPHYSICAL PUBLISHING COMPANY,
NEW YORK,
NO. 331 MADISON AVENUE.

www.ingramcontent.com/pod-product-compliance
Lightning Source LLC
Chambersburg PA
CBHW031747230426
43669CB00007B/526